Cromarty-Living by the Sea

Cromarty - Living by the Sea

*A collection of reminiscences, thoughts
and feelings about the sea*

- by the people of Cromarty -

Edited by
Fran Tilbrook

Published by
Cromarty Courthouse in association with Cromarty 2007

Edited by Fran Tilbrook

Published by Cromarty Courthouse in association with
Cromarty 2007 as part of Cromarty's 'Sea Cromarty Sparkle'
celebrations for Scotland's Year of Highland Culture.

With the financial support of
the Heritage Lottery Fund, Highland 2007 and The Cromarty Trust

ISBN 978-1-898416-84-5

Designed by It's all Good, info@itsallgood.org.uk

Printed by Biddles Ltd. www.biddles.co.uk

Financially supported by:

THE
CROMARTY
TRUST

Heritage
LOTTERY FUNDED

Cover photo: *Aerial view of Cromarty looking east through the Sutors. Courtesy of the University of Aberdeen*
Insets: *Left, Low tide sunrise. Photo by Calum Davidson*
Centre, Sea anemone and sea squirts in the Moray Firth. Photo by George Brown
Right, Cromarty harbour. Photo by Calum Davidson

Contents

Poems:

Children's voices:

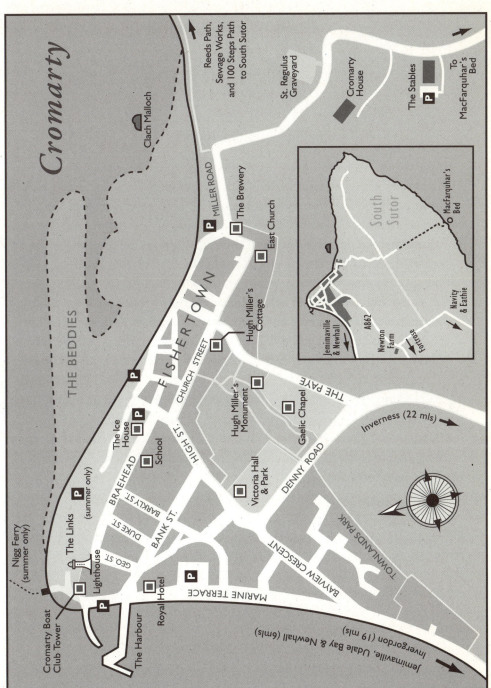

Cromarty

THE BEDDIES

Clach Malloch

Nigg Ferry
(summer only)

Cromarty Boat
Club Tower

The Links

The Harbour

Lighthouse

Royal Hotel

The Ice
House

School

BRAEHEAD

DUKE ST.

GEO. ST.

BANK ST.

BARKLY ST.

HIGH ST.

CHURCH STREET

FISHERTOWN

MILLER ROAD

The Brewery

East Church

Hugh Miller's
Cottage

Hugh Miller's
Monument

Gaelic Chapel

THE PAYE

Victoria Hall
& Park

DENNY ROAD

MARINE TERRACE

BAYVIEW CRESCENT

TOMNLANDS PARK

Inverness (22 mls)

Jemimaville, Udale Bay & Newhall (6mls)
Invergordon (19 mls)

Reeds Path,
Sewage Works,
and 100 Steps Path
to South Sutor

St. Regulus
Graveyard

Cromarty
House

The Stables

To
MacFarquhar's
Bed

(summer only)

South Sutor

MacFarquhar's
Bed

Jemimaville & Newhall

A862

Newton
Farm

Navity
& Eathie

Fortrose

Colin Dunn, Plexus Media

5

Acknowledgements

As incomers ourselves, though with 65 years between us in Cromarty, the Project Team (Fran Tilbrook, Martin Gostwick and David Ross) would like to thank the people of Cromarty for enthusiastically supporting this effort and for contributing to it in so many ways. It has been a privilege to put this collection together.

Our thanks go to the Heritage Lottery Fund, Highland 2007 and The Cromarty Trust, without whose financial support nothing would have been possible. We are very grateful to our voluntary Feedback Group: Wanda Mackay, Catriona Gillies, May Hunter, Archie Mactaggart, Fraser Thomson and Chris Faulds for their enthusiasm, helpful advice and useful input to the whole project. Thanks to Joel Mason Houck for timely advice and encouragement, to John McNaught for his assistance; to Miss Rose and the staff of Cromarty Primary School for their willing support; also to the small panel from outwith Cromarty who selected the children's work included here. Thanks to Calum Davidson and the other photographers for taking or providing so many excellent photos. We're also grateful to staff and volunteers of the WEA (Workers Educational Association), in particular to Hilary Lawson, Doraine Patience and Ann MacInnes for advice and practical assistance; to Professor Ian Russell, Director of the Elphinstone Institute, University of Aberdeen, for guidance and encouragement and to Sheena Paterson, Community Librarian, Fortrose.

Further information:
The Cromarty we knew by Eric Malcolm,
Cromarty History Society 2000.
My little town of Cromarty by David Alston, Birlinn, 2006.

Websites:
http://www.cromartylivingbythesea.co.uk Interactive website
of this book.
http://www.black-isle.info/cromarty/imagelibrary/

Photo credits for centre colour plates

Plate 1
Top: Jack-up sunrise between the Sutors *(Calum Davidson)*
Bottom: Low tide with tankers at Nigg *(Fran Tilbrook)*

Plate 2
Top: Cromarty rainbow *(Calum Davidson)*
Bottom: Cromarty peninsula *(Georgia Macleod)*

Plate 3
Top: Waders and Jemimaville *(Georgia Macleod)*
Bottom: From the 'Cursed Rock', the Clach Malloch *(Calum Davidson)*

Plate 4
Top: From the South Sutor looking west to Invergordon *(Calum Davidson)*
Left: Low tide sunrise *(Calum Davidson)*
Right: Oblivious of the cruise liner *(Calum Davidson)*
Bottom: Cromarty from the coast road *(Georgia Macleod)*

Plate 5
Left: Her first paddle in the firth *(Peter Tilbrook)*
Top right: Sea anemone and sea squirts in the Moray Firth *(George Brown)*
Mid right: Rig transporter ship with two jack-ups aboard *(Peter Tilbrook)*
Bottom: Across the Links to Nigg *(Courtesy of David Ross)*

Plate 6
Top: When the firth was full of rigs *(Calum Davidson)*
Bottom: Cromarty harbour *(Calum Davidson)*

Plate 7
Top: QM2 passes the slip *(Calum Davidson)*
Bottom: Heading out to the Sutors *(EcoVentures)*

Plate 8
Top: Lighthouse sunset *(Calum Davidson)*
Left: Enjoying the sand *(Peter Tilbrook)*
Right: Cromarty wildlife *(Calum Davidson)*

Introduction

Towards the end of 2005, people in Cromarty started discussing how the community might celebrate 'Scotland's Year of Highland Culture 2007'.

A group of volunteers *(Cromarty 2007)* soon decided to hold a summer festival of the sea, recognising Cromarty's strong and varied maritime links. Amongst the earliest proposals was an idea that seized our imaginations: to compile a collection of thoughts, memories and feelings about what the sea means, or has meant, to the people of Cromarty today.

This would be as inclusive a project as possible. It would embrace not only the memories of our oldest residents, many of whom have a long line of sea-faring ancestors and who have themselves witnessed great changes as fishing gave way to oil and tourism; but also a selection of younger voices. We wanted to hear from native-born Cromarty folk and those who have chosen to live here.

Funding from Highland 2007, the Heritage Lottery Fund and The Cromarty Trust enabled the idea to become a reality and in the autumn of 2006 the project got under way.

Posters in shop windows encouraged people to start thinking about the sea; follow-up invitations to take part were delivered to every house in the town's postal area, and the Project Team also invited key individuals to be interviewed – their words appearing in first-person accounts that form the heart of this project.

We knew we would hear some good stories. What we didn't anticipate was the breadth and depth of experiences – beside, on and under the sea and not just concerning our local shores. There are tales of accidents and near drownings, of heroic rescues, of battles against the elements, of the sea as creative inspiration as well as work provider. There is poetry and humour, philosophy and reminiscence. There are reminders of the past, when boarding the ferryboat was as commonplace as catching a bus, when the Cromarty Firth was full of huge ships whose crews filled the town's streets and parks, when the Fishertown was just that: its residents speaking their own 'patois', when giant oil rigs were constructed across the water and nowadays, of research and tourism on the same waters. From old and young alike we heard of the timeless, simple pleasures of swimming, fishing and 'harbour jumping'.

Older people knew the sea was in their blood. We hope that, by contributing to this project in so many ways, our younger residents also recognise just how great a part the sea still plays in giving them a sense of place, of community, of what makes Cromarty so special for all of us lucky enough to live here.

From the outset we decided to let people's voices speak for themselves, even if their accounts clashed with those of others. We are not historians and take no responsibility for factual errors in the various individual accounts. We were privileged to listen, to marvel at people's amazing powers of recall and to record. All three of us have thoroughly enjoyed sharing in the experiences of the contributors and we're confident that the material collected here will lead to further studies exploring other strands of Cromarty's rich oral history.

Fran Tilbrook (Project Leader), Martin Gostwick and David Ross.

Mrs Newell at home in Cromarty
Photo by Joel Mason Houck.

Jean Newell is Cromarty's oldest resident. She will be 99 in 2007 but can still close her eyes and remember Cromarty before, during and after the First World War: the huge warships that would glide in and out of the Cromarty Firth; the sailors, soldiers and early airmen on their way to the war to end all wars. She was Jean Campbell then but living in the same house as she is today, where people come and consult her on any and every question relating to Cromarty's story. She is the town's most important historical witness.

My first real memory was the Coronation of 1911 (George V and Queen Mary). All the bairns congregated outside the Royal Hotel and we marched to the Reeds Park, which was the playing field at that time. That was where the boys from HMS *Natal* were playing football when she blew up in 1915. I remember that more clearly.

I was outside the house playing with my brother when we heard the explosion and he caught me by the hand and pulled me after him. We went helter skelter down to the harbour and when we looked up the firth you could see her and all this smoke rising above the *Natal*. There were big crowds there, but I didn't really know what was happening.

I remember one of the boys from the *Natal* who was ashore saying "Oh I left my bank book on board". That would have been a big thing at that time, even if there was only two pounds in it. But another boy said "My brother was on board." It really was a terrible thing.

There were quite a lot of people to do with the *Natal* in Cromarty that day. You see when the navy used to come up, the officers' wives would come up as well and stay in Cromarty and were found grand places to stay. We had some here and I remember being asked to post a letter and it was being sent to ...something... 'Hall'. That was the address. Of course I was thinking of the Victoria Hall and I thought 'fancy staying in a hall'.

But before all that I remember playing down on the shore with Betty MacKenzie before the First World War. We were building sand castles when a flying boat stopped not very far from us and I saw two men getting out over the side and into the sea. We looked in amazement because they had boots on that seemed to come up to their waists. They must have been thigh boots. I didn't look at their faces because I was so intrigued by their boots. But I later found out their names were Oliver and Longmore.

At that time Cromarty was the only place in Britain which had a flying boat base. The shore was suitable because of the sand and it was free from rocks. As far as I remember the flying boats stayed in the water and it was the men who came ashore, but I was only a bairn. But it shows you how important Cromarty was in those days to the navy. It was Cromarty that was the home base, not Invergordon.

Mr Malcolm was the headmaster at the school when I went. He was excellent and very hard working. He did so much for his pupils. He gave us everything. He shaped our lives, gave us a love of learning all sorts of things, but not just from books. He had a tennis court marked out in the playground and would take the boys down to the Links for cricket. He was really good for Cromarty, but he always seemed to be working.

The only time he took off was a Saturday morning when he used to go over to Nigg to play golf. I can see him yet in John Skinner's ferry with his golf clubs. There were quite a few who went over. I think it was a nine-hole golf course.

He also offered evening classes in navigation and I remember Albert Watson who ran the ferry to Invergordon and was latterly lifeboat coxswain going to these classes, along with a good number of others. I think Mr Malcolm had gone to Aberdeen on a course so that he could offer these classes.

I spent the final years of school in Dingwall Academy, in the hostel. I had a great time singing at concerts. I would get the ferry across to Invergordon and then the train down to Dingwall and wouldn't get home again until the holidays. The ferry to Invergordon played a big part in all our lives. It was the main route to and from Cromarty. There were no buses.

After I had finished training as a teacher at Jordanhill College of Education in Glasgow, the first job I got was at Applecross on the west coast. To get there I had to take the ferry to Invergordon, get a train to Dingwall, then another one to Kyle of Lochalsh. Once I got there I got on the steamer that was going to Lewis. It dropped anchor off Applecross where it was met by a rowing boat, which took us ashore. It was quite a journey!

Later I got a teaching job in Invergordon. That was from about 1930 to 1937. I used to get the ferry every day at 7.30am and back again about 5pm, getting home at 5.30pm. I was a good sailor and used to be given the tiller. I could take her in alongside the pier. I became quite good at it. Indeed I remember once something happened to the boat and people said, "Well it wouldn't have been Jean Campbell who did it."

I remember the Invergordon Mutiny in 1931. When we got up to Invergordon on the ferry we could see the seamen all leaning on the railings of the battleships, doing nothing. We thought that was strange. You could also hear music, somebody playing a piano. It was clear that something had happened.

It had been announced that their pay was to be cut by 10%. I think Philip Snowden was the Chancellor of the Exchequer at the time. The cut wasn't so bad for the officers with private incomes, but the ordinary seamen had little enough as it was without getting it cut. They didn't know how on earth their families were going to feed themselves back in their home ports in the south of England. They had to do something. They refused to put to sea. Then I remember going along to Braehead to see the fleet leave after the mutiny, which only lasted a day or two. They had been called back to the south. I had such a heavy heart seeing the ships pass, these poor men now held in disgrace by the navy that I had loved so much. It was so sad.

Contrasts

by Evelyn Sutherland

5 years at Peddieston, Cromarty, remembering the seas around Shetland.

From the glittering rays of sunrise over an airless horizon throwing sparkling lights across the sea to the shore, to the moonlit rippling of the surface on a dark winter's night interrupted only by the regular sweep of the lighthouse beam and the twinkling ships' lights, the sea was a comforting partner to our island community.

It was our umbilical cord to the mainland. It put food on our tables. It provided employment. It entertained us as children. It helped forecast our weather. It gave up seaweed to provide nutrients for our land. It brought ashore timber - a valuable commodity in our treeless landscape. It carried home our relatives. It brought our visitors. It reminded us regularly of how lucky we were to be able to share it and its beauty.

The influence of the sea shaped us for the future.

Whipped by the wind the gigantic waves crashed onto our beaches, clawing furiously at our shoreline. Spume, like thick cream, was thrown high into the air to shatter into millions of droplets. The wild sea with no respect, grabbing, chasing, tossing everything in its way, taking what it wanted and spitting out what it rejected with awesome force. The sea was a respected partner to our island community.

It took away many of our loved ones. It damaged our fishing fleets. It disrupted our ferries. It forced us to ration our supplies. It put at risk the lives of our brave RNLI volunteers. It made necessary journeys uncomfortable and often dangerous. It made us anxious as we waited for news of missing persons. It reminded us regularly of just how vulnerable and weak we were when its beauty turned to anger.

The influence of the sea shaped us for the future.

Betty Hourston with her Royal Humane Society certificate.
Photo by Calum Davidson.

Betty Hourston was born 85 years ago in the same house in Cromarty's Gordon's Lane that she still lives in today.

I was born Betty Hogg on 17th September 1921. I have lived in this house all my days. I taught myself to swim, oh aye, in the sea of course. I got the corks to put round my middle from my Auntie Maggie. She was Bobby Hogg's auntie. I learnt to swim when I was about 12 – my mother was not long dead. We didn't have swimsuits in those days.

There was sewing in the schools and I'd make myself just a gingham frock and swim in that. You were maybe not all that decent. You never thought about it in those days.

I'd go in at half tide. My granny always told me not to swim out, but to swim along, because of the danger of the beddies below Hugh Miller's Monument – that stretch of sand there, when the tide was coming in that quick. It's all changed now. I'd swim all the way along from below the house to where the sewer outfall is now. I was on my own. My grandfather and father were both good swimmers. They were always in the water. They were hot summers in them days. My grandfather, Willie Hogg, would never allow me to swim on the Sabbath. I was also banned from swimming in the harbour, but I'd go there, swim, climb out at the steps below Stella Watson's office, where the Vee used to be. She was the daughter of Captain John Watson who ran the steamers then. My granda caught me in the harbour one day. I was holding on to the barnacles sticking out of the pier wall and I got a row.

Later on there were bathing huts, below the monument. This is still long before the last World War. They were where the old YMCA was. All the children would go there after school. Helen Hogg, she was one of them; Cathy Walker, she was my chum. Betty Fraser, who became a professor, she was a marvellous swimmer; Alison Malcolm, Eric's sister: these were the older ones.

When I left school at about 14, I was always in the harbour and so were a lot of the other children. I used to hide the towel under my arm from my grandfather when I wanted to swim on the Sabbath. Then I would swim in the regatta. We swam blindfold, straight across the harbour. I won some races, beating them from the baths in Inverness. They were marvellous swimmers, with all the beautiful strokes. I wasn't a good swimmer – just the breaststroke – but I was strong. I won naturally, straight from the step, on the bell, to the step on the other side. The regattas were a lot of fun, with the greasy pole and the coble racing, and that. The cobles fished right up into the 1970s.

Learning the children to swim, I used to hold them until I could get them to float. Some had more confidence than others. If I was in the water, everything was okay. "Betty, Betty", they used to shout. No life jackets or armbands or nothing. Maybe just a rope round their middle. Jock McBean was one of them. So was Bill Campbell's brother, Colin. Helen Hogg's nephew Rossie, that became a professor. Confidence was the key thing. They would know themselves when they were ready to swim.

Later on, youngsters from the school would learn at the baths in Inverness. I went with the teacher. One of the girls, a Maclean lassie, jumped in. She thought it was the shallow end but it was the deep end. She was lying to the bottom. I got her out. She has remembered it to this day, reminds me every time I see her. We'd take the Boys Brigade in the bus to the Alness baths when Mr Galloway was the minister in charge of them.

Janet Davie and I were in swimming with dolphins. We were at the old beddie and they were so close we could hear them breathing. Another time, we were swimming near the steps, on the shore below my house, and salmon rose right up in front of us. We were shouting to each other, "catch one, catch one." In these later years, 1970s, 1980s, I was teaching another generation to swim. I wouldn't say teaching, it was just giving them the confidence. They would shout, "Betty, Betty", same as when I started learning the previous generations. They're all grown up now with families of their own, they grow up that quick. I was well known for swimming to the lifeboat every day. It was moored a bit beyond where all the yachts are now.

In 1973 Betty Hogg and Nurse Jenny Ruthven were awarded the bronze medal of The Royal Humane Society and received a parchment certificate from the Queen, for saving three men employed at the Hi-Fab offshore fabrication yard at Nigg from drowning off the Cromarty foreshore. This is Betty's account of that night.

I'll never forget it. It was midnight on 13th May. I was up watching a film on TV, a Western. Then I heard shouting for help. I ran out of the house, in my nightdress, and I realised there were men in the water, three of them as it turned out, because their boat had capsized, just in front of Weatherglass House. I heard later that it had struck a piece of timber. They were returning home after a night out at Rosemarkie and their boat overturned and they panicked.

I went straight into the sea. I didn't have a second thought about it. It was just natural. You don't think of yourself. You don't think of things like you might be risking your own life. I knew what I was doing. I took the first man ashore who was in the shallows. He was sick. He said another man further out there couldn't swim, so in I went again. This second chap was in quite a state. He'd swallowed quite a lot of water and hurt his leg, so I got him out as well.

What a fright I got when I returned to the shore again and found the first man I'd rescued had gone – disappeared. I found out that he'd walked up the Little Vennel towards the light he'd seen in Paye House, which was Dr Forth's surgery then. Dr Forth called the ambulance which took the three of them away to be treated for hypothermia.

The third man had apparently got trapped in the bunghole of the boat. Nurse Ruthven found him, and Albert Watson and John Gillies, the ferrymen, got the boat out to him. There was a lot of commotion. The police were there. Anne Short contacted the Coastguard.

I got the Humane Society medal from the Lord Lieutenant of the County, Matheson of the Brahan Estate. Colonel Ross was there, and the police, and most of the village at a ceremony in the Victoria Hall. Later on, Nurse Ruthven and I got the VIP treatment at Hi-Fab: flowers, a tour of the works and all that. I'm glad to say all three men involved are still alive.

What's it like, living by the sea here? Our lives change a lot round it but the sea goes on, in all its moods.

It used to come right up into Fishertown, before the bulwark got built up. I can remember a storm when the waves and spray went right over Weatherglass House. It was during the War – some of the road got washed away. You couldn't get into the house by the front. I went up Gordon's Lane and down Miller Lane and over the garden wall to see if Granny Brown, the old lady who had a broken arm, and her daughter, Nurse Hossack, were okay. Eric Malcolm's house was always in danger, and up Miller Lane. My husband used to barricade Ron Tomlinson's and Russell House with sandbags when a flood was in the offing.

The Atlantic Fleet in the summers, they were a sight – it was the battle cruiser *Hood* always lay off Cromarty. I mind the *Hood* crew marching to the East Church and playing rugby in the cornfields. All the ships sailing out when the War was declared, the whole lot going out. The tank landing craft coming in when they were practising for the Normandy landings.

I saw the Queen when she came by sea to Cromarty in 1963. I was sitting on the wall of Lydia Cottage watching when she came to visit Hugh Miller's Cottage. Oh, she was beautiful, she was lovely, she was. Oh what a complexion she had.

I married Willy Hourston, an Orkney man, on 7th September 1974. His son Alistair met his future wife, Ginny Stokes, on our wedding day. They have had four lovely children. My grandsons Allan and Scott were both in the navy. Allan was in the Falklands. Scott served on the aircraft carrier *Illustrious*. He was at the handover of Hong Kong to the Chinese. Another boy, Joey, is a pilot officer in the RAF. Willie and I stayed on in this house, same as always. I went down to the Isle of Wight and Glasgow for short holidays, but Cromarty's the place for me.

I like salmon, the fresh salmon, nothing like it in the world. My father, James Hogg, worked for the Moray Firth Salmon Fishing Company – coble fishing. He would carry the fish all the way up from the Eathie station to Navity and then down to the ice house in Cromarty. You would get a fish at home if it had already been damaged by a seal bite, or maybe damaged some other way! If it was done by someone deliberately and he got caught, you could get the prison for that.

I like the rigs at night with the lights on like Christmas trees. Otherwise I don't care about them one way or the other. It's Cromarty by the sea. Before I go to bed, I listen to the waves and I hear the swells in my bed at night. I went down in the dark the other night to watch a big tanker coming in with all its lights on. I have seen the sea in all its moods, and they are many. My favourite swimming chum was Janet Davie. People would say, "oh it's cold", and I'd say "oh no, it's lovely and warm." I have gone on swimming to this day – I was swimming this year. I have the sea in my blood. Yes, I have always loved the water. I will till the day I die.

Waves lash Marine Terrace in the Jan 2005 storms.   Photo by Fran Tilbrook.

Living by the Sea

by Courtney

I enjoy living by the sea. It is amazing. I love the calm sea and when you skim stones it ripples away. I also love it when I can swim or paddle. I also enjoy sitting watching the sunset on a beautiful summer's night – I just think it is very romantic. When I was younger I loved running away from the waves when it came in and chasing it when it went out.

I also like taking my dog long walks along the beach and walking along myself. It keeps you fit and healthy. Also I like cycling out towards Jemimaville while the sun sets. It's brill.

In Cromarty by the sea there is always an ever-changing view. When the tide goes out the more sand it takes out and pushes lots of sand back on shore. It is spectacular. I love it when the tide is out because there is more beach to go on to run on.

I do not enjoy it when the tide is in and it is really horrid and stormy because it's very windy and wavy. I absolutely hate being cold.

The fishing boats are very beautiful but the oil rigs ruin the view as they hide things. I love sitting on the beach drawing the view ahead of me. The view is just beautiful.

I love living by the sea.

Living by the seaside _by James_

Living by the Sea is really great
I go with my Grandad to get fishing bait
Visiting dolphins they appear
I Jump into his boat and start to steer
Near the Sutors mackurel we catch
Greedy Seagulls invade our patch
Back to the harbor we take our haul
Yes we go home to share it all
Tomorrow I am playing on the beach
Having fun with my dog's I try to teach
Eating ice-cream watching waves
Salty spray in my face
Every day somthing new
Always looking at a different view

Youth Development Worker Wanda Mackay ready to kayak.
Photo courtesy of Wanda Mackay.

'Water baby' Wanda Mackay was born and brought up in Cromarty. Since 2002 she has been the town's Youth Development Worker.

I learnt to swim when I was three or four, in Fishertown where I was born and grew up – at Tigh na Mara – where Uncle Peter (Wilkinson) lives now. We lived there until I was about six, and Betty (Hourston) who lived just along the road, taught me. I suppose that would be round about the mid 1970s. I don't remember much about it, but I think it was just like she told you. She would hold me floating until I had the confidence to just do it myself.

I asked my mum about it. She said as a child I loved water from the very start. Whenever we visited any of my aunts they would put me in a basin or in the sink because I was full of devilment. I was fascinated with the water. I once put my Auntie's good watch down the toilet and flushed it. I tried to tell her: I kept saying, "clocko, clocko". My mum told me, whenever there was a blink of sun, I would be down to the sea and Betty would have me in the water. Betty would be in her mid-fifties. My dad used to put me in a dinghy and pull me along with a string from the beach.

When we moved to Bayview Crescent, I'd go down in front of the house where there's a stone bit with an iron in it: a hoop or something, where an old anchor was. You could stand on this stone, the tide coming below your feet quick and stay there a bit longer till the water came over you. I'd spend all winter down there, playing, skimming stones, and in the summer I would be swimming every day. I still do. I did all the strokes when I was young. I do the breast stroke now, though I can still do all the others. I'm a strong swimmer. Still go to the pool at Dingwall, three to five times a week and do a mile every time I go. Of course I take my son Connor with me. That's why he's doing so well and he's only eight. He's been taking lessons since he was four. Last week he completed 24 lengths. Next week he's doing his assessment for his half mile. He's not yet as confident in the sea as I was at his age, but he's getting there. I'm still swimming in the sea a fair distance out, regularly, from the harbour, out past the yachts and back. I did that several times this summer, leaving Connor with my mum.

At Cromarty Primary School we did lessons every year. I swam with the Brownies, with the Girls Brigade and the Boys Brigade. Any opportunity there was for swimming, I took it. In the summer when I came home from school, I would be straight into the water. When I was older at the Academy, I would come home and go straight for a swim before going to work at the Royal (Hotel). My mother would make me stand outside the back door in a basin of water because you were covered in sand.

Whatever it is about me, I don't feel the water cold. I've swum from Cromarty to Nigg, and that's one time I did feel a bit cold, in the middle there. When I go canoeing and canyoning with the young people, I will see them coming out cold after a couple of hours, with white lips, quivering, and I'm fine. I can be in the water for five hours and not feel it.

Why did I swim from Cromarty to Nigg? Because Sid (Maclean) had done it. Sid and his brother Ali Maclean had. I'm sure Rory Gunn swam it with me one of the times. We were young. We were told Sid had done it, so we wanted to do it. I did it just in a swimsuit – no vest, no wetsuit, no flippers. Took me two, two and a half hours. I was maybe thirteen or fourteen. There'd be a boat or two round you, in case you got cramp and they needed to haul you out. At the other side, to warm up? Sweeties and crisps. You don't think about hot drinks when you're a child.

I did the raft races, where you built your own raft, in the regattas. There'd be hundreds of people down by the seafront then.

Jim and Kate Jack ran the youth club when I was in my teens, and they organised the canoeing in the sea then. There were no child protection or safety laws that we have now, and so you didn't have to have a powerboat out in the water. Aye, there'd be lifejackets. I couldn't guarantee all of us could swim, but they didn't care as long as we had lifejackets. We would take out twelve canoes and they would make twelve of us raft together and you'd play tig. And then of course everybody would tip over the canoes and you'd all fall in. That was our favourite activity. Then there'd be canoeing right round the harbour and into the bay opposite Bayview Crescent.

Later on, I can mind water-skiing from the harbour. There was two guys came over from Invergordon who would whisk us around.

They were lively days at the Royal when I worked there, from the age of 12 till 21, 22. Then there was the fishermen bringing catches into the harbour. At the Royal, the men gave us fish and we gave them beer. It wasn't a money deal, ever. They'd have tabs for up to £20, £30. It was their dinner and their drink for the fish, which is why the hotel always had fish. Locally, it was Sid and 'Ginga' and 'Totter' that supplied everyone with fish: salmon, crabs, lobsters, many years ago before they all got caught with their nets and things tightened up.

I remember the time when all the fish was washed up on the beach which had broken loose from the fish farm. We took all the fish and sold it to the hotels in Inverness. Even the younger ones, we went after the fish. Bruce Watson, me and someone else got chased by the baillies one night out the Shore road. They got my dinghy. My own brother when he was younger used to catch lobsters, one for himself and one for the hotel.

I love salmon, lobster, crab, whelks, mussels. Christopher, my partner, says that's a Cromarty thing because he's not such a seafood lover and nor is my mum. My dad would get up and fry fish for his breakfast, as does Sid: mackerel, trout, the whole lot. Connor loves to go fishing with his dad when he comes home at weekends. He wrote quite a nice story about that for Cromarty Primary School. Mackerel and 'twiddlies'. When he catches something, his dad has to eat it.

My dad Kenneth, you know, 'Totter', many years ago worked at Nigg. One night it was the October holidays and he and the rest of his squad were working overtime. They clocked off at eight o'clock and went to the local pub, 'The Piggery', until the back-shift finished. I guess it would be about three in the morning. There was a new boat collecting them that night in the harbour. Dad went on it – obviously they were all drunk

– it was narrower at the bow, and dad just slipped off there, right into the water. He can't swim. This was October and the water was baltic. He went down and came up and down a second time. The third time he went down, he didn't think he was coming up and Brian Morrison dived in and saved his life. Later on, at Brian's silver anniversary, my dad got up and made a speech and said he was only there because of Brian.

Aye there were times when I was growing up, risking my own life without even thinking about it. Like when I was 18 or 19, on a Friday night in The Royal, when I'd be drunk and everybody used to dare me to dive off from the tin shed, swim to the harbour beach and I would – fully-dressed, drunk, no lights or nothing out there! People would buy me a drink if I'd do it, and then when everybody had bought me one, I'd go and do it. It happened regularly. I love doing things which have an element of danger to them. The things that we used to do in The Royal and the Legion, all the time. Because I'd swum the harbour for so many years, so many times, all day every day, you know, I've absolutely no fear there whatsoever. When we go abroad, I'll swim in any water: Antigua, Egypt – this year we're going to Cuba. They're all places I can get out swimming and the sea is always like a warm bath compared to Cromarty.

The Youth Club

The children of Cromarty, I believe, are so good at water-based activities because any child of Cromarty will take to the water at any opportunity from an early age. I work with children from other areas that are nowhere near as confident in the water. Canyoning is very extreme. I took 12 young people canyoning in the Meag Gorge, and I said, "only gladiators need apply." You've got to be super-confident, because there's rocks you've got to slide down, and jump into really, really fierce water, then you've got to swim aggressively to get yourself out of it, climb out and up at different bits. Kimberley, Katie, Catriona, Corrie, James, Chris, Calum, Gavin, Jordan, they were all gladiators. We have a full summer programme every year, a lot of challenge and opportunity. We abseiled down the Corrie Falls at Cannich. Shiona and Fraser were petrified but they still did it, and we've done two-day and five-day canoeing expeditions.

I have about 40 members of the club at the moment, mostly 11 to 16, sometimes up to 18, and some of them come back as volunteers. We have a junior youth café as well.

I'm chasing funding all the time for the activities, helmets, safety equipment and all the rest of it. The summer programme costs about £12,000 altogether this year. There's football and a lot of indoor sports and activities as well, but always half the expenditure goes on water-based activities. Every child between 4 and 18 gets an opportunity for something. Cromarty Action for Young People is a registered charity, and my part of it is working with teenagers and community-based work, trying to pull the generations together.

What's so special about the harbour for the kids? They're all together, know each other from school and the youth café and they go home, get their swimsuits and go straight there. There's the boats that you're not supposed to climb on, but you do. I remember me and Rory once dived off after a small wooden paddle boat which broke loose from its mooring and pulled it back into the harbour. Last summer (2006) there was the harbour jumps with the children all going in, thrown in inside the fish boxes, which was a stunt for the BBC Restoration Village programme about Cromarty and the East Church. It's what you do. It's almost bred into you. It is, it really is. You see a patch of sun and you want to be in the water.

When I feel totally stressed out, say, after a long hard week, I go for a swim, do my mile and the water's so good, I come out so refreshed, re-energised. Sparkling, yeah.

Sea Changes

by Jennifer Mactaggart

25 years in Cromarty

I miss the lighthouse. The building still stands up on the Braehead but its light has gone. There's no sudden ray to spotlight my dog as we walk the Links on winter nights. No beam lights up a segment of the Firth and there's no longer an answer from far-off Covesea.

Times change of course and so does technology but the new brighter buoys, flashing harsh red and green, seem poor substitutes. The Cromarty light was one link in the chain of Stevenson lights guarding the Scottish coastline. When we moved here from the Hebrides it offered a familiar landmark: small, sturdy and reassuring just like the one we'd left by Lochindaal in Islay.

Our twenty-five years of living by the Fishertown shore have seen other changes too. In north-easterly gales the rollers no longer pound the vertical seawall sending terrifying judders through Shore Street and up the Vennels. The bouldered sea-defences may not be beautiful but they've proved their worth. Our seaward gable once needed a protective storm shutter — not any more. Nor do spray and seaweed hit our first floor bedroom window. Best of all, the house itself has stopped shaking.

The landscape's different too. The telegraph poles have gone; the sewage pipes have been replaced by a massive concrete pumping station. Over at Nigg sections of rigs have given way to windmills. We've been here long enough to remember a time before the long jetty, before the tankers came with their lights and the night-time hum of machinery.

But in spite of the changes much remains the same. There's a constancy about the sea itself. The sounds of waves on shingle seem more natural now than silence. The late Robert Hendry told a story about Cromarty recruits to a Highland regiment. Billeted in an inland barracks, the Cromarty boys were unable to sleep for three nights until a sergeant (a Black Isle man himself) suggested throwing buckets of water at the barracks windows. According to Robert it worked. Back then we laughed at that story. Not now.

On maps and charts the distance between our shore and the North Sutor remains constant. Yet weather and conditions often suggest otherwise. Some mornings we wake to the foghorns of tugs or barges and can't even see the opposite shoreline. At other times with sunlight picking out individual sheep and yellow gorse clumps the Sutor seems to have shifted southwards in some bizarre game of Grandmother's Footsteps.

The goldeneyes no longer return to the sewer pipe each winter but the grey herons still stand by the burn mouth and the gulls are bolder than ever. We see dolphins less often nowadays so their rare appearances seem all the more special. And just once, near midnight in late June seventeen years ago, I saw an otter hunch his unhurried way down the sand to melt into the shallows…

A telescope and binoculars stand by the window. Our passing traffic goes by water: yachts, dinghies and kayaks, the lifeboat, tankers, tugs, barges and snub-nosed fishing boats. There's no need for the lighthouse tender now and we see far fewer rigs but other traffic is on the increase. In summer the liners visit so frequently we almost take them for granted – great white, picture-windowed, balconied, seagoing apartment blocks – dwarfing the tiny pilot-boat scurrying alongside.

Some still make an impact. Forty years ago I stood watching the QE2 being launched from John Brown's shipyard. Now I can stand at my window and watch her heading seawards, her bulk blocking out the Sutor.

I may not mend nets or bait lines, but there are times when I share experiences with Fishertown wives down the centuries. I too have a seagoing husband. Like them I register the rising wind and the white-flecked waves. I too have stood gazing eastwards, waiting apprehensively until a far-off speck of red-brown sail comes reassuringly closer.

When you live by the sea some things never change.

Catriona Gillies.
Photo by John McNaught.

Born in Cromarty, Catriona Gillies was the youngest of six children. For 44 years she was the town's sub postmistress and in 1992 was the last person in Britain to receive the British Empire Medal – presented by the Lord Lieutenant in Cromarty's Royal Hotel.

I have one particular memory during the war, when I was at Cromarty School, and I've never forgotten this. Mr Malcolm, the head teacher, used to take us down on to the Links for gym, for exercises. I can remember this very clearly, this plane coming in the Sutors, flying over our heads and it went past, we didn't know where it went, but anyway I would say not ten minutes after that it came back and it went back out the Sutors. And what do you think that plane did? It came to bomb the oil tanks at the Royal Navy base at Invergordon but missed the target. And we were all on the Links. We didn't know anything until the next day. You didn't know then what was happening until it was on the radio the next morning. I remember saying to somebody at school, "that was the plane that flew over - that was a German plane going over our heads". You know, you could almost touch it, it was so low, just over our heads. I don't know if anyone else remembers it.

After the war, when I finished school in Cromarty, I didn't want to go to Fortrose Academy, and I was offered a job with the Bank of Scotland in Cromarty. But my sister Florence was with the Post Office and I really wanted to go and work for the Post Office too. Anyway, my sister was asked by the Dingwall Head Office if she would go and work in Dingwall and I went to work in the Cromarty Post Office and

HRH Duchess of Gloucester visits Cromarty in 1956 to name the new Lifeboat. As an RNLI supporter, Catriona can be seen, bottom right of the picture, wearing a special uniform hat.
Photo courtesy of Catriona Gillies.

that's where I stayed. When I started, the Postmistress in Cromarty was Morag Campbell. They were desperately needing somebody to work in Invergordon for a few weeks, so I went every morning to Invergordon at about 7a.m., getting back about 6p.m. – it was quite a long day. They were very nice at Invergordon. I used to travel each day on Albert Watson's ferry boat from Cromarty to Invergordon, all on my own. Albert was such a wonderful sailor, really, but it could be very rough. And in fact, when I would come home at night and go to bed, my head was filled with the motion of the boat, but it's amazing, I never felt sick; just that feeling when I went to bed that I was still on the ferry!

Just before I started there were two postmen, Hugh and Evan. The mail came over from Invergordon on the ferry. They would take a little barrow, go down to the harbour and pick up the mail which would come in about half past nine in the morning. But the first mail would leave Cromarty at half past seven to go to Invergordon and one of the postmen would have to take that down to the ferry. Then when Albert Watson gave up the ferry they had to find another way of getting the mail to Inverness, so after 1969 it went by bus to Fortrose where it was picked up and went right through to Inverness. Just after my brother John started as the postman, he got a post office van.

There was always a fishery cruiser coming into the Firth. They always used to come in and collect their mail – we would keep it for them if they were going to be up here for any length of time. I always remember Captain Owen, captain of the *Longa*. There was the *Longa,* the *Brenda* and the *Freya:* fishery cruisers going back and fore to Cromarty from Leith. A lot of the men who were on the *Longa* belonged to Leith. Fishery cruisers would look after the waters of the Firth, see that nothing untoward was going on: protection duties, you might say. They were terribly nice and kind. Every Christmas I would get this huge box of chocolates from the captain and crew and I was invited out to tea with them on board, which was lovely. Bigger ships would also come in and ask us out there for tea. We'd get dressed up, certainly. Actually, when big ships like the *Courageous* came in, people were always invited – it was like an open day. They would send in the pinnaces to pick people up and take them out on board. And I can even remember when I was at school, going out to the *Courageous* with our headmaster, Mr Malcolm. The *Courageous* was very much part of Cromarty. Some of the officers would give us a tour of the ship. We were all on our best behaviour. Many years later the sailors would ask if we could organise a dance for them in the Victoria Hall, and they would all come to the dance – and sometimes they would bring their own band.

How did I get involved with the RNLI? I would be maybe 18. There was a notice up, I think, asking for people to go along to a meeting at the Hugh Miller Institute. Mrs Ross of Cromarty was the President. There weren't very many there, I remember. As time went on we had various sales and afternoon teas. Effie Mackay from Farness took over as Secretary and later, Phyllis Hardie. We had sales of work, tables down at the harbour – the Lifeboat was based here in those days, with Albert as Coxswain.

I always remember when the Duchess of Gloucester came in 1956 to name what was to be Cromarty's last lifeboat, the *Lilla Marras, Douglas*

Plate 1

See page 7 for captions and credits

Plate 2

See page 7 for captions and credits

Plate 3

See page 7 for captions and credits

Plate 4

See page 7 for captions and credits

Plate 5

See page 7 for captions and credits

Plate 6

See page 7 for captions and credits

Plate 7

See page 7 for captions and credits

Plate 8

See page 7 for captions and credits

and Will. When the Lifeboat was taken up to Invergordon it was very sad for Cromarty. Albert's son Clem Watson, now retired, became the Area Organiser for the North of Scotland RNLI. I was President of the Ladies Guild for some time and have enjoyed being involved for over fifty years – I'm still involved!

When I was in the Post Office I started collecting old postcards of Cromarty. The little bits that are written on the back are so interesting. I have one with the date: 4th September 1905: 'This is a bonny place, quite different from anything I have seen before.' It was posted in Cromarty 101 years ago. And another one postmarked 1905 with a picture of the *Saga*, a very famous boat in Cromarty.

We loved the sea, that's where we went in the summertime. We would all go down and sit, quite a few of us, just sit down on the shore – we didn't go and sit in the garden. We were drawn to the sea and people still go and sit by the sea if it's a lovely day. I don't think I could ever go away from here.

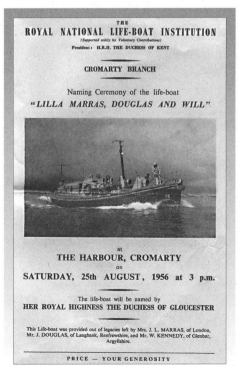

Naming ceremony programme for Lilla Marras, Douglas & Will, Cromarty's last lifeboat. .
Courtesy of Babs Mackay.

At night the waves grow high
they get higher and higher, they never seem to die
they crash a gainst the wall
they try to make it fall

they keep on crashing
they never stop that constant lashing
they try to get over the wall, to flood
Get streets all wet turn earth to mud

but in the morning the sea makes no sound
the streets are wet and so is the ground

by Finlay

Clem Watson completing his kayak trip from Invergordon in aid of the Victoria Hall. Courtesy of Clem Watson.

Born and bred in Cromarty, Clem Watson left the town in 1962 and now lives in Nairn. However, his links with Cromarty remain as strong as ever and he is a regular contributor to the Cromarty Image Library. Son of the legendary Albert Watson and grandson of John Watson, Clem has a vast store of memories (and memorabilia) about the town and its maritime heritage.

Others will have mentioned my father, Albert Watson's, businesses in Cromarty – the ferry to Invergordon and the coal and mail delivery businesses. But what of the family tradition of service with the Cromarty lifeboat?

My grandfather, John Watson, set the trend by saving 72 lives at sea in various parts of the world and served as coxswain of the Cromarty lifeboat from 1917 to 1933. My father took over from him as coxswain in 1933 and served in that capacity for 35 years. My uncle John was also the lifeboat's first mechanic, serving 45 years. They were both involved in one of the lifeboat's most dramatic rescues on the evening of 7th December 1959.

The Cromarty lifeboat at the time was the *Lilla Marras, Douglas and Will,* a 46'-9" wooden Watson. She launched to the aid of a stricken coaster adrift in the Moray Firth shortly before high water at 4.45 pm. The *Servus,* a vessel of 360 gross tons from Leith, was some 40 miles from the lifeboat station. Normally in the Moray Firth area the wind seems to increase with the start of the ebb tide, so just after the lifeboat got underway, the wind increased to a full gale. The lifeboat rolled heavily on its way to the search area. Buckie lifeboat had been out that day and returned, and Wick could not launch as conditions were too severe.

The fishery cruiser *Explorer* was spotted at 1.30 a.m., and after a radio conversation between lifeboat and fishery cruiser, the exact position of the casualty was ascertained and contact made. The *Servus* was then inside the 20-fathom line, a mile offshore and eight miles WSW of Clythness lighthouse. She was lying head to sea with two anchors down, yawing violently and ranging on her chains as the severe gale swept her shoreward at a speed of one knot.

My father, Coxswain Albert Watson, brought the lifeboat ahead of the coaster and down her port side, turned sharply and approached her port quarter. Through the fury of the spray, five of the eight-man crew jumped to the safety of the lifeboat deck.

The sea was so fierce there was no chance to use ropes. Quick action of helm and full astern engine power of the twin diesels prevented the lifeboat being swept on to the top of the cargo hold. Waves at this time were 15 to 20ft high, so a second run in was made to the same position on the *Servus'* port quarter and the remaining three jumped to safety.

The rescue, after contact with the *Servus,* lasted some 20 minutes, and at 2 a.m. the lifeboat left the coaster and made for Cromarty, which was reached at 7.45 a.m. For this service the RNLI's Silver Medal for gallantry was awarded to my father, the Bronze Medal to his brother, Mechanic John Watson, and thanks on Vellum to Assistant Mechanic George Morrison. Remaining crew were given Medal Service Certificates.

The coaster ran aground just below Dunbeath Castle rocks on the Caithness coast and became a total wreck. I have some press cuttings and one cites Captain Pirie of *Servus* saying: "Never have I seen better handling of a boat. It was superb seamanship". My Uncle John said of the *Lilla Marras,* "It was her first really big test and she came through it with flying colours."

Despite battling with heavy seas for 15 hours, my father immediately transferred into his own boat to do the regular, three times a day, 5-mile crossing to Invergordon with the mail, for which dedication to duty he received a special letter of thanks from the Head Postmaster in Inverness. However, it was a letter from the daughter of one of the rescued that overwhelmed my father. It simply said, "Thank you for saving my Daddy".

Lifeboat board in the East Church porch, commemorating many rescues, including that of the M.V. Servus.
Photo by Calum Davidson.

To celebrate my 65th birthday in 2001 I decided to kayak from Invergordon to Cromarty. This was partly in tribute to my father's memory, and partly for old times' sake (as from the age of fourteen I often ran the ferry boat on my own to Invergordon and back to help my father). It took me precisely one hour and raised £1200 for the Victoria Hall.

Before retiring, I worked for many years as the north of Scotland fundraiser for the RNLI. The RNLI, a voluntary organisation, is committed to be 50 miles offshore within 2½ hours. To be able to maintain that sort of operational capacity, it's essential to have good lifeboats, capable of withstanding all sorts of storms such as that experienced in the account above by Cromarty's last lifeboat, the *Lilla Marras,* in 1959. Sadly, Cromarty lost its Lifeboat Station in 1968 when the Coastal Revenue Committee of the RNLI took the decision to close it, based on the decline in coastal shipping in the 1960s. Then with the arrival of the North Sea Oil activity in 1972, the same Committee had a further look at sea safety provision. By that time Cromarty had lost most of its men to the Nigg Yard – thus nobody left to crew a lifeboat here, and the new lifeboat was placed at Invergordon. The Station re-opened there in 1974.

Finally, here are some memories of my childhood in Cromarty: setting a scanty of about 400 hooks to catch flat fish in Udale Bay, fishing from the pier, going out with 'Big Robert' to Guillam Bank to catch cod and staying in the salmon bothy overnight with the fishers for an opportunity to assist with the catch at about 4a.m. What a wonderful happy time in the great outdoors was had by all of my peers at that time. In winter we helped collect the ice, in large lumps, off the Navity Pools just above Newton. Ice was loaded into horse carts and small lorries and transported to the ice house on Braehead, to be used in June, July and August to chill the salmon going to London by rail from Invergordon, via my father's ferry. We were aye working, with pleasure, and ending up with 6d in old money (2½p nowadays!)

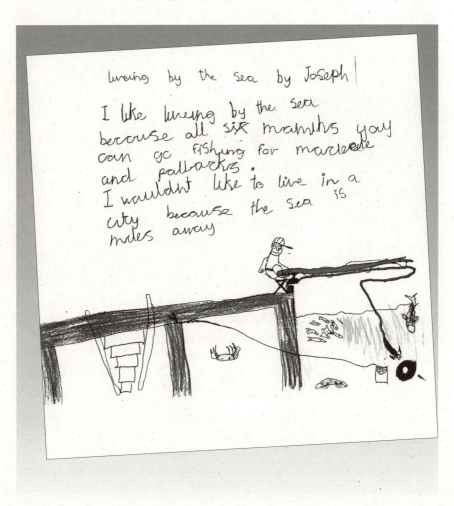

Living by the Sea

by Catriona

The white horse, grey rough sea,
The gusts of wind scattering the leaves,
The old townsfolk getting all the 'gass',
The sound of fishing boats sailing into harbour.

The white horse, grey rough sea,
The waves hurtling in,
The patient seagulls drifting away
On top of the rough sea.

The gusts of wind scattering the leaves,
The wind banging on my windows,
The rain howling across the firth
And spreading like a disease.

I love living by the sea,
The peace is priceless…

Babs Mackay.
Photo by John McNaught.

Babs Mackay (87) lived in Church Street in Cromarty for much of her life. As a child her house was 2 Church Street and she was later to run a draper's shop across the road beside Struy House where she lived until recently, latterly with her daughter Moira and her family.

Almost exactly 70 years ago her late husband Jack was involved in a dramatic rescue in the waters of the Moray Firth, for which he was honoured – just one episode from her life spent beside the sea.

We used to love swimming at the Links and down at the harbour. There was a bathing hut down from the lighthouse on the Links, just a wee bit up from the shore. The sand was beautiful down there. There was also a bathing hut out on the shore road on the other side of the harbour but I can't remember exactly where. We used to love swimming. We would just run straight in.

The summers seemed much warmer. We would run barefoot everywhere. We would fish at the harbour and go beachcombing, looking for shells and fossils.

That reminds me of the story about Mary Maclean, a Cromarty businesswoman who owned and ran the local laundry and was my mother's first cousin. She employed local people and was known as Mary Hoochty. She also kept goats on the Links and would give their milk to mothers with delicate children.

She would go down to the Links to feed the goats and then would go beachcombing. One day she came across a box which she thought would make an ideal seat for beside the fire. She carried it back to her home where Sutor Creek is now. However somebody had already seen the same box and knew it contained explosives and had gone to fetch the local policeman, Sergeant Hume. Luckily Mary had been spotted and Sergeant Hume went to her house and found her sitting on the box beside her fire. He very quickly removed the box and took it away to the Police Station. She was pretty lucky.

Of course we had a regatta every year with swimming and diving competitions. If you walk down the harbour there is a big V and that's where we used to do the diving and we would swim out from there. There was a greasy pole. I didn't do it but my husband did. We were all young. There was rowing. Eric Malcolm's two sisters and Bobby Hogg's two sisters used to do the rowing. There were boats for couples and for fours. I think they used to get the boats from the salmon fishers. There was also a pontoon in the harbour for the Highland dancers and that's where the regatta queen would be crowned. The lifeboat would also give us trips. Of course we had the lifeboat station in Cromarty as well.

The Watson family had a boat called the *Ailsa* and used to take people over to the Nairn Games and sightseeing. She was a lovely ship. They also had the *Endeavour* and the *Enterprise*. They would go up and down to Invergordon, leaving here at 7.30 in the morning, 11.30a.m., and 3.30p.m. They never charged much for passengers because they had the mail contract. If it was a very stormy winter and the roads were blocked Cromarty was fortunate because we would get our mail from Invergordon along with our papers and goods for the shops. But the rest of the Black Isle would be stuck. We had a lot to do with Invergordon. We could go over and catch the train or the bus down south. But when the Watsons lost the Royal Mail contract they couldn't carry on.

Of course there was also a ferry to Nigg. That was run by Gracie's father, John Skinner. We would go across to the sands at Nigg for Sunday school picnics and the like. That was a great day out. There was also a golf course and there would be a few people would go across to play – Eric Malcolm's father and the doctor and some others. We would also go for picnics to MacFarquhar's Bed. Practically all we did was to walk about and I would pay somebody £100 a day to get me walking like that again.

But there was always a lot of activity in the firth. The coal would come in by boat and there was a shed at the top of the harbour for the excise men. Don't remember much about that. But I do remember watching the salmon fishermen at work. They would have their nets out at weekends so they could mend them. When they took their fish in they would store them beside Bob Cherry's house.

We also used to watch the women baiting the fishing lines for the fishermen and carrying the men out to their boats, but that has been well recorded.

Before the war my late husband Jack was involved in what a newspaper described as an amazing rescue in the Moray Firth. I have the cutting here. He was just 17 and was working at the harvest at Navity Farm along with another two men, Donald Macfarlane and George Finlayson, when they noticed a plane in difficulties. Both the occupants jumped out. One parachute opened and the other fixed on the tail of the plane.

The paper said the men rushed to the seashore, down over the steep cliffs. Mackay and Finlayson swam out to the plane and got the airman extracted from his parachute. Mackay then turned the officer over and, using the life-saving method, swam with him until Finlayson got a rope from MacFarlane on the shore. Mackay tied the rope round the airman and got him ashore and over the rocks. Mackay was slightly bruised by the rocks when landing.

They carried the airman to the salmon fishers' bothy. Captain Morison and others arrived from Navity Farm and rendered first aid. Local doctors and nurses came soon afterwards and helped revive the pilot. The rescued officer was Pilot Flying Officer Duncan Whiteley Balden, attached to HMS *Courageous*. He was taken on board a destroyer which had sped to the scene.

The paper finished by saying that the gallant men who swam out to the rescue fully clothed were fortunately none the worse for their thrilling experience.

The men were later guests of Admiral Royle RN and the officers of HMS *Courageous* and spent a day at sea on the aircraft carrier.

Miss Molly Morison of Navity later married Flight Lieut. Balden on

Cromarty Lads Rescue Airman From Firth

A SEAPLANE of No. 800 Fleet Fighter Squadron, from the aircraft carrier Courageous, fell into the sea at Moray Firth yesterday.

The pilot, Flying Officer Duncan Whitely Balden, was rescued by two Cromarty lads, but the passenger, First Class Aircraftman John Beresford Murfin, lost his life.

Three aeroplanes from the Courageous were carrying out flying practice when one of them was seen to be in difficulties. It nose-dived from 3000 feet.

Harvesters at work in the field at Navity Farm, Cromarty, rushed to the shore. Two men were seen to jump with parachutes from the 'plane. One of them fell into the sea.

Down 250 Feet Cliff

Two Cromarty lads, George Finlayson and Jack Mackay, harvesting at Navity, ran from the field, descended a 250-ft. cliff, and rushed into the sea fully clothed. They swam to the airman, who was struggling in the water with his parachute, and effected a thrilling rescue.

The airman was unconscious when the lads took him ashore. Artificial respiration was applied by Captain Douglas Morison, of Navity, and members of his household. The airman partially recovered and was taken aboard a destroyer which drew into the shore and sent a boat off for him.

Body Recovered

The other airman's parachute failed to function, and he was seen hurtling towards earth. A search, which continued over several hours, was made by police, airmen, and many aeroplanes from the Courageous and the air base at Novar.

The observer hurtled in the direction of the Eathie Burn, about two and a half miles from Cromarty, in wild country. The body was recovered lying among bracken behind the Eathie salmon fishers' bothy.

The wrecked 'plane was located close to the shore, between two and three miles from Cromarty.

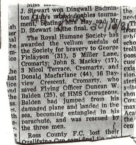

to Mr Maclennan. A handbag to Mrs Maclennan and a pearl necklace to the youngest girl.

An interesting ceremony took place at Cromarty, when three men — George Finlayson, John Mackay and Donald Macfarlane — were presented with vellum certificates of the Royal Humane Society in recognition of bravery.

The men were harvesting at Navity, when they saw a plane crash in the Firth from a height of 3,000ft. In their rush to the rescue, they descended a precipitous 200ft. cliff and swam to the wrecked plane, where they found the pilot entangled in his parachute. He was unconscious when brought ashore, but responded to artificial respiration. The presentation took place in the Victoria Hall, which was packed for the occasion. Provost D. R. Mackenzie presided, and handed over the certificates. Among those who spoke were the King's Harbourmaster at Invergordon; Flt.-Cmdr. Fairweather, RAF Evanton; Captain D. Morison, Navity; and Baillie D. Malcolm.

The Rev. Donald Macdonald, [...] has been [...]

Press clippings from 1938 describing Jack Mackay's rescue of a pilot off Navity.
Courtesy of Babs Mackay

J. Stewart won Dingwall Badminton Club's mixed doubles tournament, beating [...] Hay and Mr D. Stewart in the final. 30/10/81

The Royal Humane Society has awarded the vellum medals of the Society for bravery to George Finlayson (31), 5 Miller Lane, Cromarty; John S. Mackay (17), 3 Nicol Terrace, Cromarty, and Donald Macfarlane (44), 16 Bayview Crescent, Cromarty, who saved Flying Officer Duncan W. Balden (25), of HMS Courageous. Balden had jumped from his damaged plane and landed in the sea, becoming entangled in his parachute, and was rescued by the three men.

Ross County F.C. lost their Qualifying Cup [...]

3rd Sept 1938 in the East Church in Cromarty. The three men were invited to the wedding and later received Royal Humane Society Award Certificates.

At the start of the war I remember seeing a plane with a swastika that flew between the Sutors right up to Invergordon and bombed one of the oil tanks and we were mesmerised. That was in the early days of the war and we didn't realise what was happening. I think Betty Hogg saw it as well.

It is funny to remember that during the war all the mail from Cromarty was checked, because of all the military activity round here. But if you gave mail to one of the soldiers going into Inverness to post, it wouldn't be. If you went by the bus to Muir of Ord you would get searched but if you went across the ferry and got the train, you weren't searched. It really was pretty stupid.

The Queen was here twice and it was by Nigg she came and all the children were lined up at the harbour. She walked right from the harbour to Hugh Miller's Cottage. Then the next time she came here to review the fleet in the firth. The fleet would come in May and September each year for about six weeks. There would be the *Hood*, the *Renown*, the *Repulse, Courageous, Ark Royal* – all the different boats. What a sight it was to see their lights at night. The whole firth would be lit up. They would be out at sea during the week doing their exercises but came back in at weekends when most of the ships were open to the public so you could go out and get on board. The sailors would come ashore to play football. So would their bands and they were wonderful, very entertaining. They would start at the harbour and march round the town.

My late husband Jack served with the 4th Battalion of the Seaforth Highlands, 51st Highland Division and was captured at St Valery in 1940, aged 20. He was a prisoner of war for five years. After he was liberated by the Americans he came home, reaching Cromarty on 16th May 1945 on Albert Watson's ferry boat. Johnnie Aird was waiting on the pier to welcome Jack home (Johnnie did this for all the POW lads returning home). He played the pipes, leading Jack all the way to his home at Nicol Terrace.

"When you're born in a place where you're looking out at the sea, it's naturally a part of you"

(Jean Macbeath)

"I'm fascinated by the comings and goings on the Firth. In a small way it was part of the pull and attraction of moving here. At that time there were at least 14 rigs sparkling dangerously during the winter nights. We fantasised that they were alien space stations."

(Susan Christie)

Coral Star, the ferry used by hundreds of Cromarty oil-rig workers travelling to Nigg's Hi-Fab Yard. One of her skippers was Billy Watson whose family own this painting.
Photo by Calum Davidson.

Retired motor engineer Billy Watson is 68. Born in Shore Street, with seafarers among his forebears, he has sailed all the seas in all the weathers round Britain.

My father's father, James, was a yawl line fisherman who drowned in the Moray Firth some time between the wars. My maternal grandfather was a fisherman too. But I didn't go to sea at first. I served my time as an engineer at Andersons garage in Dingwall, then drove buses: Highland Omnibuses.

I became the Cromarty lifeboat's engineer – the only full-time member of the crew – in 1963, in my mid-twenties, and continued until the station closed in 1968. This was the last Cromarty lifeboat, the *Lilla Marras, Douglas & Will;* she succeeded *The Brothers* and the *James Macfee,* and when last heard of was still on the waters – of Dutch canals (see *The Cromarty We Knew,* by Eric Malcolm).

The *Lilla Marras* was a Watson Class boat, a 48-footer with a crew of 8; she had two 40hp diesel engines and could make 8 knots. She came to Cromarty brand new in the mid-50s, built in Cowes, Isle of Wight. She was a fine boat, a typical lifeboat. In the five years I served as her engineer the boat wasn't called out in an emergency, but I kept her ready to sail, round the clock and year round. When she was at sea I operated the engines with my second engineer, Ronnie Winton, with the coxs'n shouting at us, "pull ahead", "go astern", and all that.

I would check the boat, carry out the maintenance, at least once a day, ensure she was ready to sail at all times. It would take me maybe a couple of hours. A lot of it was polishing all that brass – all the engine controls were brass. The rest of the crew took that part of it all for granted. We had the district engineer twice a year and the lifeboat inspectors once or twice a year to check things up.

Nearly 40 years later I can still remember the names of many of the volunteers: the coxswain Albert Watson, second coxswain Eddie Scott, second engineer Ronnie Winton, Billie Bathie, Jimmy 'Mallaig' Hossack, Willie 'Skip' Mackay, Alistair Maclean.

I did occasional runs for the Invergordon ferry/mail boats, the *Enterprise* and the *Endeavour*, and overhauled them. They were owned and run by the *Lilla Marras*' coxswain, Albert Watson (no relation), son of the famous Captain Watson of the 1930s steamboat, the *Ailsa*. They were 36ft motorboats with Kelvin engines which never had a breakdown on my runs. They were always afloat except for the annual overhaul that would take just over a week.

On that ferry run Albert was the 'delivery man' for all the goods for Cromarty's shops, and all the booze – barrels and barrels of beer and bottles for the pubs.

I also served as harbourmaster in those years. That was when we had the coal boats coming in, four ships a year, with cargoes of 100-odd tons a time. The fuel was transported from ship to large storage depots in the town, one being what's now Donald Macintosh's work shed and another one situated down by the present-day surgery. We used to have coasters coming in too, with sacks of fertiliser slag for the farmers.

Like the harbourmasters before and since I did not wear a uniform. My job was to catch the boat-ropes, tie them up and collect their dues – dues that went into the coffers of the Cromarty Harbour Trust.

When the Cromarty lifeboat closed I carried on till 1970 with overhauling lifeboats from stations all over the country, usually sailing them to, and working on them, at Buckie. I shifted boats all over the place. We used to take a relief boat from one station to Buckie, then take their boat back, then the relief boat to somewhere else, and so on.

Stornoway, Longhope (Orkney), Kirkwall, Aberdeen, Anstruther, Fraserburgh – their boats came to Buckie. The west coast boats, the Barra, Islay boats, I would take to Sandbank on the Clyde.

Then I was on an experimental boat for a year, the first of the fibreglass fast boats – that was doing valuation trials, didn't matter what the weather was, seven days a week at sea, to value what the boat was going to do. That lasted for a whole year, going round all the different stations, all round the coasts of Britain. She was known as the 40-doubleO-1. (40-00-1).

So I suppose you could say I was a key man in proving the first fibreglass boats of the kind familiar today, aye. The pay wasn't good. I got a letter of thanks for saving a guy in a small boat who ran aground off Sheerness in the Thames at three o'clock in the morning. The 40-doubleO-1 had finished her trials, and I was on board while they trained the crew up.

When I finished with the lifeboats I was taken on, together with John Patience from Avoch, as skipper/engineer of the Nigg Yard shiftworkers' ferry and did that for 13 years, from 1972 to 1984. I sailed five boats in all: the *Petersham*, the *Reaper*, the *Queen of Scots*, the *Sutor's Last*, and finally the *Coral Star*. They were all diesel engines. The last one, the *Coral Star*, was a 70-footer with Yankee engines, Detroit diesels, 500 horse-power. She could carry up to 150 passengers.

I've no stories about those years, even though I was transporting hundreds of yard workers to and from work. There were a few drunk sometimes. But I knew who they were and they were never any trouble.

It was on the *Coral Star*, after she had finished her Cromarty-Nigg runs, that I had my one and only life-threatening experience at sea. We were taking her to Arbroath, the skipper and me, when we nearly lost her in a storm. She was filling up with water and kept filling, even with all the pumps going, and the buckets, and when we reached Arbroath the next day we found she'd had her bilge keels ripped off. The skipper didn't put a May Day out. We were lucky. I thought she'd go down. She was sold to a man called Alec Mann and went back to sea.

I spent my final working years back on land. I finished at Mackays Garage in Dingwall as a heavy maintenance fitter. I started out in a Dingwall garage and ended up back in a Dingwall garage. That's quite funny. I'm one of those they call Cromarty's 'Pier Parliament' – we gather at the harbour and share the craic.

Do I think that global warming could one day cause the seas to rise and change the face of Cromarty? I always say, life changes, and that's that. I take it as it comes.

There's a model of the latest lifeboat, the Severn Class, sitting on a shelf in Billy's house. It's not a souvenir of service – it was won by his wife Fiona in a raffle.

The Fright of My Life

by Archie Mactaggart

25 years in Cromarty

The *Hen Harrier* was almost new. Made of white pine planks on larch frames, she was the penultimate Greencastle skiff built by the late Gilbert Clark of Port Charlotte, Islay. She was 24 feet long with a sharp stern, light but strong, a craft of great beauty built by an extraordinary man using the materials he cut from 'bends' sent from forests on the mainland and planks prepared in his own superb workshop overlooking Lochindaal. The experience gained over a lifetime combined with the patience of a craftsman to build a boat that smelled lovely and looked lovely and touched everyone who entered the workshop – and not a plan in sight. It seemed half the village filed into the shop on a daily basis, not to gauge progress but because the conversation was always scintillating and often hilarious – Gilbert was a wordsmith without equal.

When I took delivery of her I could hardly wait to get the *Hen Harrier* to sea. She had the dubious distinction of being the first sea-angling boat grant aided by the Highlands and Islands Development Board. Once in the water she had a grace I have never seen matched, exemplifying the saying about boats – "If she looks right then she is right". In early June we went fishing night after night in all weathers, getting great catches: sometimes cod and always mackerel but especially haddock, plump ones about three pounds in weight. All the time getting to know one another, I quickly worked up a trust in her and the single cylinder Lister diesel which had the skiff cantering along at six knots while only sipping fuel in the process – I doubt if she was as happy with my performance.

Bob Early, who fitted her stern gear, owned a shark rod and tackle. He had attempted, unsuccessfully, to catch sharks in the North Channel between Islay and Ireland, dangerous waters with all sorts of races. When a tide changed without warning these would suddenly manifest themselves in huge standing waves which terrified the inexperienced and sometimes the experienced.

Even then I knew I was foolish to buy Bob's rod. With hindsight I think it was the vicious looking hook about six inches long that attracted my interest, but as soon as I clinched the deal I started looking round for a crew.

An obvious choice was Bill Syme, who in his time had hunted big game in India, mature and unflappable. Jimmy Mainland, an Orcadian, the local lighthouse keeper coming up to retirement after a lifetime in the service and an excellent fisherman, agreed to come as well. As I had only three rods I reckoned that was enough.

We agreed that we would head out at the first spell of settled weather to arrive in the North Channel at slack water just before the ebb which flows south. We would fish for a couple of hours so that we would head for home before the tide got too strong. All these plans were based on Admiralty Charts and Cruising Club data because our local knowledge was nil. What we did have was a fund of stories of catastrophes and narrow squeaks that encouraged us to temper our hopes for our day out with a great deal of caution.

To complement our array of rods, hooks and fearsome homemade instruments designed to retrieve our prey, I had arranged for a dustbin full of blood from the local slaughterhouse to 'chum' the water to attract our quarry. It was deemed an essential lure irresistible to any sharks that might be cruising in the vicinity.

It did not enter my mind at that stage that the shark as a species is reputedly able to detect blood in the water twenty miles out and might therefore arrive at our chosen spot in force. My thinking was more along the lines that a single shark – not too small and certainly not too big - would respond to the stimulus of a couple of buckets of blood tipped over the side by presenting himself to take the bait, minded to being spiked and hooked aboard. Then I got down to the difficult problem of arranging for our food and drink for the next day. As the weather was really settled and my chosen companions were available – the choice of Chablis for the salmon pâté seemed inspired!

Crawford Anderson, a Church of Scotland minister, a larger than life individual and a good friend who was holidaying with us, insisted on joining us. Then Iain Gillespie, a vet, also asked if he could come along.

We set sail from Port Charlotte pier with everything checked, double-checked and with spirits at a high, I suppose by bravado whipped up by feelings of self satisfaction and large surges of testosterone. The sea was like glass and we had the morning sun full on us bearing down from a cloudless sky. The pipes were out and the scent of tobacco added to our sense of well being. We had eight miles to go so we pointed the bow between the Mull of Oa and the Rhinns. To get fresh bait for our hooks we would stop and catch a dozen mackerel off the hamlet of Nerabus.

Seating arrangements on the skiff were four seats in front of the engine and one abaft for the man at the tiller who looked forward while the rest of the complement looked out over the stern. Iain was in the bow seat, then Jimmy Mainland, then Bill Syme, then me with the dustbin of blood between my legs just in front of the engine. Before we left, Crawford had insisted that he wanted to steer; as it was such a lovely day he got his wish.

Crawford was in top form and pulling my leg mercilessly as was his wont, his face split with a perpetual grin. Suddenly – we were about half a mile away from our first stop – Crawford gave a shout: "Shark!" and pointed. We all looked round but could see nothing. I got immediately on my high horse and in sentences liberally laced with the "F" word which I knew he hated, told Crawford that it was well known that ministers were bad luck on boats, especially on fishing trips, and if he didn't stop his caper he would be landed. Crawford was still protesting as I shut down the engine when we had arrived off Nerabus and we lay about one thousand yards off shore.

We got out our line frames and started to lower our 'darraghs' which were hit at once by mackerel. We were all pulling them in when all of a sudden, not a hundred yards away, not fifty, not twenty, but ten yards away the sea parted and a huge black head broke the surface, moving at right angles to our stern. The creature's eye seemed to be the size of a saucer and that eye was definitely looking directly at me. It exhaled with a sigh, then disappeared beneath the sea, its spear-like fin at least four feet high slicing the haze left from the exhalation.

What our faces looked like to Crawford after the creature disappeared – he saw nothing and was unaware of the source of the dissipating dampness enveloping him – must have been interesting. Now my reflexes kicked in, driven by sheer terror. My voice in the highest of falsettos squeaked "What was that?" There was no immediate response from my friends behind me.

When Jimmy Mainland – veteran of a lifetime spent in small boats – offered after what seemed an age "Was it a porpoise?" I found myself galvanized into action. "Chuck the lines over the side!" I squealed, starting the engine and shrieking at the puzzled Crawford to head for the shore.

The gap between the *Hen Harrier* and the shore seemed miles wide.

I expected the attack to come at any second. I had no doubt that the creature had already decided that I – with the dustbin of blood between my legs – should head the menu. It crossed my mind to ask Crawford to change places with me but he was a lot bigger than me and catching on quickly to our predicament. To get him to move would have required a lot of force and, what was worse, a loss of face in front of the rest of the crew.

Fear does peculiar things to the mind. The skiff had seemed to flit across the water as we left the pier but now she was acting like an old tub just making headway and no more. My companions seemed calm though a bit pale and in complete denial about what we had experienced. I, on the other hand, was fighting off hysteria and seemed to be heading for a full-blown heart attack, exacerbated by the dustbin and my conviction that the attack was about to explode.

We reached the tiny beach beneath my house at Nerabus, the tide enabling us to charge up the beach with the engine at full throttle. We scrambled ashore and instantly all four of us relieved ourselves in unison on the grass, much to the minister's dismay.

The dustbin of blood was quickly lifted out of the skiff and emptied on the grass well above the tideline.

By now we were exhilarated by our narrow escape and unanimously decided to cancel our trip, sitting down in the sun to eat our early lunch. I have never enjoyed anything so much. I relaxed on the machair grass with relief flooding over me, yet at the same time I relived the horrors we had just experienced. After a couple of hours' sunbathing we thought it would be safe to head for home so we loaded ourselves back on to the *Hen Harrier* and hugged the shore until we arrived safely home, appreciative and thoroughly chastened.

From the moment the head submerged behind the boat, although we were scanning all horizons, we never saw it again. The creature was a lone killer whale, a species which had never been recorded as attacking a human being up to that time. With the benefit of hindsight and my later contact with dolphins up here, the look it gave me was probably benign and not threatening.

That was the end of my shark fishing. But the shark hook is still hanging in the shed to remind me that pride comes before a fall.

Sea Change

by Jane Verburg
2½ years in Cromarty

Do you know what it's like to live with the sea in your hair,
inside your head, knitted into your sleep?

Its noiselessness, noisiness, tied to your fingertips,
its seaweed rolled in strandlines strung to your toes,
its thumbprint pebbles caught in the curve of your turn,
its sea glass in your pickets,
its curlews lifting in wide ribbons wrapped
in the palm of your hand.

Do you? Do you? I do.

Northerly Shores

by Graham Sutherland

5 years at Peddieston, Cromarty

I was brought up within a stone's throw of the sea. I used to delight in doing just that from our small garden, occasionally to the consternation of our immediate neighbour whose roof I sometimes threw the stones over! There were many in the community who relied directly or indirectly on the sea to provide employment. Whether they were family or friends it gave an acute awareness of the sea's impact on all local life.

Like all island exiles it is easy to romanticise as the flashbacks of long northern summer days fill your mind. Visions of blue skies and bluer seas and a pleasant breeze come flooding back. Memories of hours spent out in an open boat, sailing or fishing can dim those of dramatic winter storms and dark days that create a deep respect for the power of the ocean.

The sea provokes a gamut of emotions and attitudes and I can remember very clearly some occasions that created these.

My love of the sea comes from innumerable events but mainly from days spent around the islands with my father and my brothers and sisters sailing our small traditional Shetland boat. If we were not sailing, especially at local regattas, the other regular pastime was fishing as this provided food for both summer and winter.

Summer was definitely better as you ate what you caught fresh, very fresh. The variety of available fish was extensive. It included haddock, cod, ling, saithe, mackerel, not to mention shellfish and wild salmon. Fishing was mainly handline, either inside the sheltered 'voes' or out in open water at prized localities. The location of these places was jealously guarded within families and found by using visual bearings from prominent local features. One variety of shellfish we caught was the 'spoot' or razor-shell that could only be caught at very low tides in sandy areas. This required great stealth but properly cooked they were delicious. In view of the need for low tides any low, or significant spring tide, was usually referred to locally as a 'spoot ebb'. Spoots are, I believe, known in the Cromarty Firth area and in Orkney.

Winter evokes a different memory, that of salt fish. The summer catch was salted before being air dried and then hung inside. Whilst being a welcome addition to most family's larder it was not, in truth, the most exciting of fare.

Real fear was an emotion felt rarely, I am glad to say. However, being caught out alone one moonlit night in a small flat-bottomed rowing boat as the wind rapidly backed and freshened and the failure of the Shetland equivalent of a rowlock, resulted in a very nervous time. As the waves grew in size and with an inhospitable cliff now a lea shore I was fortunate to effect a temporary repair. This gave me the opportunity to get back to safety with a quartering sea to keep my adrenalin flowing. I did not grudge the long walk home but I blessed the moonlight which gave me the chance to make it and to contemplate what might have been.

Amazement came from witnessing phenomena such as the 'mareel', the local word for the phosphorescent glow produced by tiny organisms in the sea. This was particularly evident as darkness fell. Seeing myriads of sparkling water drops fall from fishing lines or oars and the boat's wake in the sea alive with an eerie luminescence is permanently etched in my memory.

Misunderstanding was an experience from my very young days. Porpoises were very regularly seen breaking the surface with a sharp and explosive intake of air before slipping back below the surface in one smooth action. As they appeared to present a semi-circular profile I believed for years that they were actually completely round in shape!

One principle emotion has to be respect. No one who experiences the sea's moods and power can ever treat it lightly. To witness huge waves coming in unchecked from the open Atlantic and pounding the shore in hurricane force winds; to see large wrecks reduced to a few sheets and beams of steel before slipping out of sight below the waves; or to marvel at massive boulders being tossed around in the surf as if they were pebbles, is an awesome experience.

The sea has generated many more memories than these. It supports a huge diversity of life with amazing bird, fish and mammals around and in it, all of which bring so many memories. It provided a highway which allowed me to travel away from the islands to work and, like so many others, took me back to my family time and time again.

I feel privileged to have enjoyed its many aspects, and to have grown up with unlimited views of the open Atlantic and North Sea for years is a bonus.

Paul Thompson.
Photo courtesy of Paul Thompson

Paul Thompson has been researching marine mammal behaviour and ecology for 20 years. He is currently Professor in the University of Aberdeen's School of Biological Sciences and Director of the Lighthouse Field Station, Cromarty, which he set up in 1989.

I grew up on the north Kent coast, just outside Whitstable. We couldn't actually see the sea from home, but it was just a two-minute walk and you were on the beach. A rather boring beach, looking back, but we spent a lot of time in, by and on the sea. The north Kent coast was a great spot for birds, particularly wintering waders and geese on the mudflats and fields. From the age of eleven or so I did lots of bird watching, and it was this interest in birds that led me to study biology at University.

Now, it's difficult to divorce my strong passion for the sea from an equally strong passion for living in Scotland. The Moray Firth coast is a very special place, but I have to admit my favourite places are small islands. Perhaps the Moray Firth is a half way house between the Thames Estuary where I grew up, and those more rugged coasts of the western and northern isles. I've been lucky enough to visit some wonderful beaches in other parts of the world, but Scottish coastlines really take some beating; not just for their wildlife interest but as places to reflect, enjoy and relax.

When I first moved to Scotland in 1982, I lived in a wonderfully remote area on the north coast of Islay. The following year I moved to Orkney, which at first seemed rather busy after Islay. On Orkney, you're rarely more than a stone's throw away from a farmhouse or a fence, and you don't have the same extensive wild hills that you get on the west. Instead, you've really got to be on the water to get that wilderness feeling. Luckily, that's exactly what my work involved. I had access to a boat and we spent much of our time out on the water. I also managed to see the whole of the coast of Orkney during several helicopter surveys which was quite a privilege.

And so to seals. While on Islay I'd been trying to get a post studying birds but I ended up working on marine mammals. At that time only two or three people had carried out UK- based PhDs in marine mammal ecology. Prior to that, anyone wanting to get into the field really had to go overseas. Things have certainly changed since then, as Cromarty alone has now produced fifteen PhD students, and each year Aberdeen, St Andrew's and several other universities produce scores of graduates who've experienced research in this area. In contrast, when I applied for my PhD – to study harbour (common) seals – my main qualification was that I'd lived on an island and was used to living in remote areas!

Although a PhD student at Aberdeen, my project was largely based with the Sea Mammal Research Unit which later moved to the University of St Andrews. They had lots of experience of working with grey seals which remain ashore during the breeding season and, whilst they aren't easy to handle, at least generally stay put. But when it came to harbour seals, much less was known about them and they were difficult to catch and handle; so some colleagues thought we wouldn't be able to catch, tag and track them. It's still not easy, but now people are routinely putting radios and data-loggers on these animals and following them around.

Most of my work has been applied research – in relation to management or conservation issues. Much of my PhD in Orkney involved working out how many harbour seals there were in that population. We're still struggling to reliably count many marine species. Ultimately we want to see how the numbers of animals change over time and what's causing those changes; but that's difficult if you can't count them effectively. Seals have the advantage over fish and dolphins as they do at least lie on the beach for much of their time. But we have to find out the best time to count them, for example when the number of seals ashore is most predictable? Then we need to work out how much of each seal's time is spent ashore, so we can adjust counts to allow for those seals still in the water. That's where the radio transmitters come in, as they can be used to work out whether each seal is resting on the beach or diving at sea. And the tags can also be used to find out where they were going when they were in the water.

More recently, people have used satellite tags, where the tag on the seal is detected by a satellite and you can sit at your computer and download the data via the internet. But "in the old days" it was a case of using a VHF radio tag – a bit like a CB radio. We used to wander around the coast with what looked like a television aerial, listening for seals. In Orkney in the early 1980s a lot of people were very sensitive about radioactivity. I later heard rumours that I was suspected of prospecting for uranium whereas I was listening for missing seals! On the beach you lose the signal when a tagged seal is less than 10kms away, but if you get higher, up a hill or in a plane, you can hear them from much further. In Eynhallow Sound in Orkney we'd be able to watch tagged seals on the beach, and hear the signal, and then track them swimming out to sea. But then they'd go round a corner and the signal would get weaker and weaker before disappearing into this 'black hole'. They may have only been going a mile or so around the corner under a cliff, or twenty miles offshore, but at that stage we simply didn't know.

In 1987 the government contracted the University of Aberdeen to do a three-year study on harbour seals in the Moray Firth. This was largely driven by the age-old controversy between seals and salmon fishermen, but also aimed to provide background information on number of seals, where they were feeding and what they were eating. It was then, when I moved down to the Moray Firth from Orkney, that our work focused more on seals' feeding habits. One of the exciting things about working in the Moray Firth is that the seals that rest on the sandbanks in the inner firths are never far from land when they head off to sea to feed. And they can't easily disappear around a headland as they'd done in Orkney. This meant that 99% of the time, from somewhere on a hill around the Moray Firth, you could find your animals. So this was the first time that we started to get a picture of where harbour seals were going to feed.

As to the conclusion of that three-year study, it's probably best summed up as "things are a lot more complicated than most people think". When we know very little, it's easy to have preconceived ideas about what's happening and how simple the system is. And then, as you gradually start to understand the animals and the ecosystem, life gets a lot more complex. The problem with applied science questions is that, so often, you tend not to produce nice clear precise answers. There's huge uncertainty over many issues. Even if we could show what seals were eating last year, that doesn't mean we can predict with certainty what will happen next year. Especially as the fish stocks could be very different from year to year. Our work showed that seals eat many different fish and other species like squid and octopus. They certainly don't spend all their time eating salmon; neither do they spend all their time hanging around the mouths of the salmon rivers. They do come into the inner firths to rest and have their pups but they're generally going much further out to sea to feed.

In the last year or so a new Moray Firth Seal Management Plan has been developed, with all the Salmon District Fishery Boards working together. This has drastically reduced the number of seals being shot in the area, and the plan focuses any control in those areas where seals are most likely to have an impact – particularly when they start moving into the rivers or feeding around river mouths. There's now a growing understanding of those interactions, but it probably takes a generation to change the culture underlying this kind of management problem. But now, most salmon fishery managers realise that improving the breeding habitat in rivers is probably a more effective way of improving salmon catches than shooting half the seals using the local haul-out site.

Dolphins have been seen in the Moray Firth since the late 1800's, but they were really beginning to capture the public's imagination at the time we arrived here in 1987. Conventional wisdom amongst the scientific community was that cetaceans were too unpredictable to do any useful research around the UK, so most work on cetacean ecology was either done overseas or based on dead animals. But when out in the boat working with the seals we often used to see the dolphins, especially around the mouth of the Cromarty Firth.

By 1989 we'd realised there was potential to do more work with the dolphins. It was known from organisations such as the Mammal Society's Cetacean Group that the Moray Firth was one of a couple of places in the UK where you regularly saw bottlenose dolphins. At that time it was thought that there were maybe 15 or 20 animals – in other words the number of dolphins that people saw on any one occasion. So the first

Dolphins off Cromarty. Photo by EcoVentures (Craig Morris)

thing we did that summer was to get a bunch of people together, standing on different bits of the coast on the same day. We were lucky. The weather was fine, and by comparing the notes that everybody took from different places, it was clear that there were at least 60 – 65 dolphins in the area. At about the same time we started going out in the boat to see if we could photograph animals and recognise different individuals by their dorsal fin (photo-ID).

Lots of classic studies have highlighted the value of basing ecological studies on known individuals rather than anonymous animals within a population. In some cases animals such as birds can be caught and marked. In the case of dolphins we can recognise different individuals from their natural marks. Recently, these long term studies of individuals have been especially useful to help understand the effects of climate change. As well as the dolphin and seal projects which we started in the

Moray Firth, the Field Station has inherited a long term study of fulmars in Orkney. Aberdeen University started this study in 1950, so we've over fifty years of data to explore how changes in climate and fisheries affect these seabird populations.

With over fifteen years of data on dolphins in the firth, we are now also seeing evidence of changes, for example in social behaviour and movements, which seem to be related to climate variation. But working out what's really causing these changes is difficult. We assume they're being driven by changes in food, and climate variation is affecting them through changes in plankton and fish stocks. But in the case of the fulmars, we don't know where they feed. Compared with many other species, we know a lot about seabird population change but much of this is based on studies at their breeding colonies – not when they're at sea. Similarly, much of our understanding relates to the summer breeding season and less is known about what they're up to during the rest of the year.

When finding out where animals go to feed, seals certainly have the advantage. They can carry relatively large tags and have hair that we can glue the tags to. Similar work on dolphins in the firth is impossible as you can't attach tags to them and, for birds, the tags have to be really tiny. Having said that, the technology is getting there, and seabird biologists in Canada have now put satellite tags on fulmars in the Arctic, showing that birds flew right across the Atlantic during the winter. So our birds in Scotland, and even the birds breeding around the Cromarty Firth, could be wintering around Greenland, Iceland or down in the southern North Sea. Hopefully in the next few years we'll have a much better picture of this.

As with so many jobs, as time goes on I spend more and more time behind a computer. It's still great to get out there with the animals, you don't want to lose that, but even at the computer I can still get excited about the data. I do miss the hands-on work that we used to do with the seals – the weighing, measuring and assessing health - and then releasing the tagged animals we'd track over the following weeks. That work ended in 1995, so it's been fun to be doing more work like this with the seabirds in recent years.

Like our annual estimates of the number of dolphins in the firth, each year we count the number of fulmars nesting on Eynhallow. To count the birds we just go up for a weekend in late May and I've got the answer. But to work out the number of dolphins, you need three people and a boat, making around twenty photo-ID surveys over the summer, and then one person spending most of the winter analysing those photographs. Then, all being well, after much number crunching you've got the number; which is why it can be difficult to persuade many ecologists that it's worth doing research on those animals!

Over the years my work has given me many memorable experiences. Last summer I was able to do surveys on the west coast, combining research and family holiday. It was my wife Sarah's birthday, and we were taking the boat across the Minch after a night on Eigg. We'd been round the coast of Rum, and at the west end of Canna a basking shark suddenly breached in front of us. It flew right out of the water, just like those Great White Sharks on 'Planet Earth'! We got half way across the Minch when all of a sudden we were surrounded by about fifty common dolphins. I'd never seen a large group of common dolphins before and they were absolutely frantic. They seem so tiny compared with the bottlenose dolphins here, especially the calves which looked about the size of rabbits. They'd rush around together and then break off into little groups, speeding off about a quarter of a mile away before suddenly returning to the boat.

Another memorable moment with dolphins in the Moray Firth occurred soon after we arrived. We were out trying to catch seals. It was at the time that we were starting to realise that dolphins were here quite regularly. We were just heading out between the Sutors when these two animals – I guess they were bow-riding the boat – were coming up either side of the Zodiac. Surfacing so close to the boat they were splashing us. But there have been many days like that when the animals have been working round the boat, so close that you can see what's happening under water.

There have also been some great moments watching dolphins from Chanonry Point or unexpectedly spotting a group when you're on the shore at Eathie. Chanonry is now so well known for dolphins that it can be incredibly busy during the summer − you can be down there with 100 or even 150 other people. I've been pretty privileged, going to remote places and being able to go out with our own boat to get a remoter wildlife experience. I suppose the challenge is to try to find ways of allowing more people to have that valuable experience with the sea and wildlife without it starting to spoil the experience or damage the environment. That's one of the issues being addressed with the new Scottish Marine Wildlife Watching Code, and the Dolphin Space Programme.

Managing wildlife watching is just one of the challenges facing us in the Moray Firth. Across the North Sea we're seeing major changes in plankton communities and fish populations and the implications for marine mammals and seabirds are far from clear. What's causing this − is it climate change, is it fishing pressure or pollution? And even if we knew the answer to that question, what opportunities are there for restoring what used to be such rich waters around our coasts? I'd like to think that we can leave the Moray Firth looking more like the west of Scotland than the Thames estuary, but the future is far from certain and it's largely down to those of us who live around its shores to shape its fate.

Each year The Cromarty Arts Trust provides month-long residencies for artists to live and work in the community. In 2006 Cromarty was privileged to welcome **Hanna Tuulikki**, whose project 'Airs of the Sea' chimed with the aims of our 2007 project. Here are some extracts from her project diary.

…This afternoon I walked to the top of the hill they call The Sutor. On either side the sea glistened and as the sun drew closer to the water it lit a path of gold. The distant waves rippled silver and the strange oil rigs seemed to lose their ominous presence. The sky is so vast here with grey and white clouds that expand in patterns across the blue.

…For over 700 years Cromarty's livelihood has depended on its proximity to the sea. The sea here is a guardian providing work for fishermen, tradesmen and more recently for the extracting of oil. The sea is a powerful mother, a repository of our deepest fears and aspirations. I want to work with the ideas of the sea because of how it has shaped Cromarty and its people.

…The rhythm of our breath parallels the rhythm of the waves. As I sit upon the rocks on the shore I breathe in the sea air and the sound of the water. The wave lifts and rises up towards the land and breaks. I breathe out. It draws near and with the mass of sea behind, is pulled back again. I breathe in.

…The breathing waves are continuous, a constant sound that lived long before the tides of traffic sound that dominate today's soundscape. But the rhythms and pitches of the sea change, as do the voices. That is, the harmony created by many voices that rise and fall, water on water and water on land.

…An idea for a piece to work on here has been growing: a sound piece replicating the sounds of the sea and the waves lapping the shore. The materials for this will be the breaths/voices of the local community.

…This morning I was up early to visit MacFarquhar's Bed. The huge archway is a mouth into the sea, nature's own palace. Barnacles covering the surface of the rocks hissed quietly as the water evaporated, a big black shag swooped past, its massive wings beating the air loudly and a pair of terns chattered playfully. The sea was calm, the water almost still as if patiently waiting for something. I put my headphones on and placed my microphone on one of the rocks jutting out into the water. The water began to swell on either side of the rock and in both ears the waves moved backwards and forwards in and out of sync with one another.

…As I stare out at the North Sutor the evening rays fall softly on to the distant form, accentuating its curves and crevices. For a moment it takes on human form and the rounded hollow now cast in shadow becomes its mouth. As the yellow sun vanishes it takes its final breath and dusk turns the giant back to rock.

…I have begun to understand the recordings of people's breath as self-portraits from the inside — the most intimate thing I can ask of somebody. I have been collecting 100 different breaths from across the community in Cromarty. From these I have sculpted a sound piece imitating the sounds of the sea and the rhythms of the waves.

(Drawn portraits of the participants were also exhibited as part of Hanna's installation.)

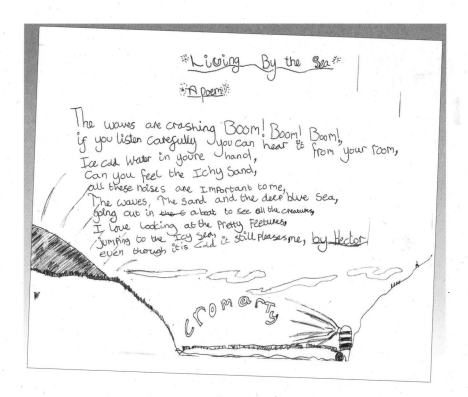

Sarah Pern skippering an EcoVentures trip from Cromarty.
Photo by Peter Tilbrook

Locally-born Sarah Pern is the owner of EcoVentures. She skippers the 9.5m RIB (rigid inflatable boat) *Saorsa* (Gaelic for 'Freedom') offering boat trips from Cromarty out into the Firth so that visitors can experience the wildlife, scenery and history of this Special Area of Conservation.

I've always had a passion for the sea, or more specifically boats. I've been fascinated by them my whole life and my most special times, memories, places and people usually involve a boat of some description! It began when aged two I was old enough to accompany my Dad out in the Firth in his old fishing boat *Choice*. He spent many years as a lobster fisherman but unusually is a keen sailor too and this he also passed on to me.

I think anyone who spends a lot of time on the water and loves the sea soon develops an interest in the wildlife that you encounter along the way. That interest for me was ultimately to develop into a business. My interest in cetaceans and wildlife tourism really began when I worked for Dolphin Ecosse whilst at home from University. I had studied Naval Architecture and Small Craft Engineering but on finishing decided that for the time being I was actually happier on the sea rather than in an office.

For me the other huge attraction of the sea is that it allows you privileged access to some of the last few wild places left in the world. There are so few places and experiences left that are not altered or made easy by human interference. I spent a few winters crewing yachts to places such as Antarctica, South Georgia, the Falklands, Brazil and Tierra del Fuego. These were incredible experiences and I will always feel very lucky to have been able to do it and to see some of these special places before they change or disappear completely.

After doing some skippering around Skye I returned to Cromarty. I suppose I had always wanted to establish a business close to home, a business that combined my love of boats and my interest in wildlife and in 2005 that opportunity presented itself and EcoVentures was launched.

We always tell people on our trips that there are no guaranteed wildlife sightings, but that we hope to see the resident colony of bottlenose dolphins, harbour porpoise, common & grey seals and even the occasional minke whale.

If conditions allow, we use a hydrophone to listen in underwater. This last summer (2006) with the calmer weather, there were some great opportunities for listening in to the dolphins - we picked up a variety of vocalisations which added a whole new dimension to the trips.

We also saw large numbers of harbour porpoise, often known as 'puffing pigs' on account of the noise made as they exhale. Unlike the dolphins they tend to keep themselves to themselves — they're shy wee things and I think often tend to get a bit overlooked. It's quite usual to get a few glimpses of minkes throughout the summer, but we saw over twelve in one day last year - more than we sometimes see in a whole year and they could be seen lunge feeding in as far as the harbour in Cromarty. We are also starting to see more unusual visitors such as sunfish and basking sharks.

It is very important to me that we run our trips in a responsible, sustainable way. I feel it is an enormous privilege to have what we do have on our doorstep here. We follow a voluntary code of conduct designed to safeguard the welfare of all the cetaceans in the Moray Firth. Accredited operators like us follow strict guidelines when approaching the animals and this ensures that any disturbance is reduced to a minimum. The dolphins become used to the regular pattern of our boat and approach only if they choose and are never pursued or harried in any way. In other words, we visit the wildlife on its own terms. Sometimes we must be content with just a glimpse or simply be happy with the knowledge that they are not there purely for our pleasure but are free to go about their business as they please.

I am a little girl called Emily
who loves living by the
sea. I love being able to go down
to the beach whenever I want to
collect stones and shells. The beach
where I love in Cromarty, has lots o
sand, we have sandcasthe
competitions in the summer whieh
is veally good fun I like
sunbathing with my mum and
brothers gary, and jamie.
we go down to the beach to
watch for Dolphins jumping
in and out of the water
my bream is that I would
like to swim whith the
Dolphins. living by the
sea is so much fun

Dolphins

I like living by the sea because I
see the sun reflecting on the water
so I can get to the beach quicker
and I make sand castles.
Erin

Robbie and Janet Davie.
Photo by Calum Davidson.

Although Robbie Davie was born in Broughty Ferry, his mother's family – Hogg – goes back at least eight generations in Cromarty. The family moved here in 1970 and he and Janet reflect on their various experiences of working with the sea – or in Robbie's case, mostly under it.

I noticed something many moons ago: the number of native oyster shells on the beach and never ever a whole one. And there was a substantial oyster fishery once in the firth and unfortunately it was over-fished. The oysters went down to London. This is a subject that interested me. That's why I started growing oysters, because I knew they'd grow. I didn't know why they died until much later. There was a severe winter – I've forgotten the year, but there was tremendous mortality of shellfish that exist in shallow water, so that's the source of most of the oyster shells on the beach. They also suffered from an oyster 'drill', a wee beastie that drills a hole. Quite often if you pick up a dead oyster shell down there (they're muckle great big oysters), you'll find a beautifully drilled round hole in them and that's oyster drill. And that's desperate news for an oyster fishery normally but I think the drills can occur at a low level without a lot of damage.

It was about 1979, 1980 when I thought I'd buy a few tiny oysters and see if they'd grow. I had no reason to think they wouldn't and they grew very well. But I didn't use native oysters, I used oysters that come from the Far East initially. They're used all over the world because they're very fast growing, they're good acceptable oysters. And they grew like stink. So I thought, let's buy a few more of them. And so I expanded to quite a big oyster farm. In order to keep them away from this 'drill' you've got to take them off the sea bed, so you make trestles and you put the oysters in bags from which they can't escape but which allows water ingress easily and tie them on to the trestles and let mother nature do the rest. You don't have to feed them – they get what they need from the sea: there's good tidal movement here and it's a safe spot.

I bought four small factory units in Dingwall and we worked away – we were selling for 10, 11 years – nearly £1 million a year turnover. We were buying in all sorts of stuff from all over the place as well as our own farmed shellfish but we finished the business about 15 years ago.

I've tried to get other people involved because there's actually pots of money to be made and it's interesting if you're that way inclined. And there's loads of capital available from HIE and the likes but there's a dearth of enthusiasm, of entrepreneurs. And that's what's essential: you've got to be wishing to make a bob and not everybody is.

The good thing in my life I've discovered is that when conditions are really tough, that's when you get most fun. When it's howling gales and people are being blown off their feet and the boat's almost sinking, that's when it's fun – that's the times you remember.

Once when I was diving for scallops I had a really scary moment. My pal and I were diving in Loch Eriboll and we'd had a very successful day. You fill your sack of scallops and tail it behind you as you're diving and as it fills up it becomes quite heavy and it becomes almost too heavy to lift to the surface, so what you do – you have a wee bag, so you take your mouthpiece out, you fill the bag with air, you tie the bag to the bag of scallops and up you go. But if you've been so greedy that you've sucked the last breath of air out of the bottle and then you try to fill the bag and you're 80ft down…which is exactly what I did – that was a scary moment.

I had a real fright once – out here – we were diving on a wreck of a coaster, out into the firth. It was a sunny day and calm when we set out. We went out in this silly little boat, about 8 miles from Cromarty into the sea. We found our wreck, which had been marked for us by the RAF. We dived into what was supposedly only 40ft of water but the ship had scoured and the thing was about 30ft deeper than that, which wasn't a problem. What was curious that day was the stratification – the different temperature layers – with completely different life situations in each layer. You could dive and suddenly it was clear and you could see for 50 yards and then you went down another two or three feet and it was solid green algae. From that point of view it was one of the most interesting dives I've ever experienced.

Then we went for the wreck – to see what we could pinch, because the thing had been sunk deliberately – it was a wartime wreck and aboard it was a fairly valuable cargo of half processed lumps of manganese. The 45-gallon drums had disappeared, so all we had were piles of these things with all sorts of beasties growing all over them. So I'm diving along here with my pal – and we'd thrown over (I'm ashamed to say) an anchor about 18 inches wide, a wee three-pronged thing that we'd found somewhere – it was flat calm. Anyway I suddenly saw this 'dust' kicking up and I thought 'What the heck?' and I realised the anchor was trailing loose. So I swam like mad for it, got up and discovered a gale had gotten up – not a clue of that down below. My pal was still down there, totally unaware of what I was doing. I got back, got the boat started and found him, which wasn't quite as simple as it sounds. All I could see of him were bubbles. However, back we came and that was a very close shave! We were empty-handed of course. Anyway, we'd decided the job was too big for us.

During the war my Dad was off, successfully winning the war single-handedly, so my Mum would come up to Cromarty to be with her family. So we spent the summer here and quite often went to school here as well, and then when my Mum got fed up we'd go back to Broughty Ferry and went to school there of course. When I was a boy, not only did I know everyone in the place, everybody was related and they all knew it. I mean people who were distant relations still realised that you were related. That doesn't occur nowadays.

I always played by the sea as a boy. My brother and I played on the beach, on the pier, swimming, never away from water. Water's always fascinated me: freshwater as well as salt. I couldn't live anywhere unless there was water nearby – I couldn't live for a minute in the desert.

I decided initially to start trying to grow a few fish in the sea. There were no fish farms of any description on the whole east coast of Britain. The first ones had started on the west. I built a couple of wooden cages along at Newhall Smiddy and put them out to sea and put some trout in them and the first ones we put out there – this was a learning experience – were too small and they promptly died or went through the net even, they were so small. I was impatient to get them in the sea. I ordered another lot and we went and got them from a fish farm at Moniack, near Beauly. I decided I'd take them back in a largish container: a lot of fish about 4-5 inches long, lovely little fat rainbow trout. So I got this container on the trailer, bought the fish, filled the container on the back of the trailer and only then realised that a cubic metre of water weighs a tonne! The whole thing just collapsed! However, we saved that situation; we retrieved the fish, got them in plastic bags which we scooted oxygen into, hustled them back here, into the boat, got them out, into the sea and we had no mortalities whatsoever.

But I had made an error, a mooring error. The cage moved, the nets got torn and the fish skedaddled. This was a couple of years before the famous 'fish-on-the-beach' episode! Then I met up with a guy, an estate owner who was growing salmon smolts to put in the sea. He had smolts and nowhere to put them. I had a site and a cage or two so we got together and we put them in and then we decided to build a lot more cages – about 12 wooden ones. And that was quite successful and then we decided that as there was public money available from the HIDB, we'd build steel cages. I think we had 18 big cages and by this time we'd decided to concentrate on trout. The blacksmiths at Newhall built them – a super job – and we pulled them out and moored them out there and when people saw the fish ashore, that was the result of a gale. I was going to say it was a combination of ice and gale but it wasn't.

The one time we had a real fright and we hadn't had the big cages in long, we had a very, very cold winter and Udale, as it used to (I haven't seen it for a long time) froze. And it froze and froze and froze and the ice came further and further out. I thought to myself, 'when this ice decides to move, it's just going to take all the cages with it'. You're talking about 100 acres of ice. That was a definite worry. We actually contemplated getting hold of hand grenades to break the ice, long before it got to the cages, obviously! But it didn't come near. When it did decide to go it rattled its way along the shore, thank goodness.

The fish that everyone remembers coming ashore were in cages due north of Shoremills. Because of the storm, one cage full of fish was washed up below the Industrial Estate units at Whitedykes. Everybody in the north of Scotland came to help themselves. It was Cromarty's very own 'Whisky Galore'. We replaced the whole lot. We were doing the trout fish farming at the same time as the shellfish business. We carried on with the mussels and oysters a lot longer – it was a separate business. If my grandfather had been alive at the same time as I was interested in this, it would have been the biggest oyster farm in Europe because he was a very go-ahead, progressive guy. My grandfather was Bobby Hogg's father.

Janet Davie: In the beginning I was very involved with the businesses. I tied hundreds of mussel ropes and sorted out oysters – all the horrible work I had to do! I suppose that's a real link with the Cromarty fisher folk in the past. I do miss the fish and the business and all that. There was always some sort of excitement going on; there was always somebody here, loads of people about us.

Launching a boat was good fun. Robert and James and one or two more helpers built this boat themselves out at the Smithy – purpose built from aluminium for the mussels. We had a proper boat-launching in the harbour and I smashed a bottle of wine against it, it was great fun – we had balloons everywhere. The first boat that we ever had was wooden and that was just for fun. It had oars but a motor as well. We fixed it all up and we'd go out and sit in the firth on nice Sundays and listen to 'Lord of the Rings' which was on the radio at the time. And one time we went over to Nigg in it to collect cockles and we got stranded! The tide went out and we were there for hours, waiting for the tide to turn. My sister was staying with us at the time and we had her children with us. And they were so worried! And we'd swim off our boat over there. We found this super, deep, deep pool – I think it's called the 'Kettle Pool' – course you can't really go there now because they challenge you and ask you what you're doing over there – it's on the oil terminal side of the jetty. It may not be there any more. I miss having a boat. I miss pottering about.

We both still swim, out at Shoremills. Robert swam end of May to about October in 2006. It's much nicer in the sea than in a pool. We're not bothered by the cold. I don't like not being able to see through the water, though – I don't like it when it's cloudy. I like to see where I'm going and I don't like to swim into great loads of seaweed or anything. Betty Hourston and I used to swim a lot, in the harbour and all over, really. We swam in a thunderstorm once. I would hate to live away from the sea, or by water, anyway. I've lived near Weston-super-Mare, so that was the sea. But we did live by a river in Oxfordshire – we've always had access to rivers or the sea. I'm hoping I'll go swimming again this summer if it's nice weather.

Living by The Sea
I Like Living by the sea becouse we get to collect Sea Shedls. and sea Snailes, herbit crabs and rock Fish. You always get to collect sticks and seaweed you always get to ae Swimming by the harbour and fishing for macKral and podlies or of your lucky you might cach salmon or cod. you might be lucky to get crabbs or spiders.

Calum

Changing Moods and Hidden Depths

the lure of the sea by Peter Tilbrook
31 years in Cromarty

Wat is it about that blue, grey or green sheet, sometimes silky-smooth, sometimes crumpled, often stretching to a horizontal line at infinity, that I find so beguiling?

Certainly, growing up in a landlocked part of the outer London sprawl means that it's not ingrained from youth. Indeed, childhood visits to the seaside were very rare, but even then I remember the thrill of that first glimpse of 'the blue line' – goose pimples of excitement. And when finally running down the beach, neither cold water nor salt in the nose killed the fascination.

My next interaction was later in life, getting out on the water through dinghy sailing. Cutting through real waves on a plane in my little12 ft boat produced an adrenalin rush, and the regular capsizing and awareness of one's vulnerability in this hostile medium engendered a respect for its power and danger.

Long oceanic journeys as a researcher in the Antarctic also made their mark. Ploughing through the southern ocean in small ships for up to three weeks at a time with only the sea and its occasional wildlife for company provided some memorable moments – experiencing the huge swell during storms in the Drake Passage for example, feeling the spray on my face while up on the deck above the bridge as we plunged into the troughs and crashed through each crest; or gliding serenely between huge icebergs, sometimes miles across and dwarfing us below their cliffs or cracking through ice flows, admittedly of modest thickness, in ice-breaker fashion.

This was where the real love affair with the sea began: on an Antarctic Base. Two and a half years living in a wooden hut just a stone's throw above the high tide mark in a sheltered bay in the South Orkney Islands sealed my attachment. Against a backdrop of snow-capped mountains the sea provided the daily spectacle, demonstrating its moods: from mirror-calm to ruffled annoyance, to raging spume-strewn gale and seasonally through frazil and pancake ice to solid sea-ice (on which we could walk or sledge or make holes and fish through) only for this to be broken up by gales into pack ice. The occasional movement of icebergs in and out of the picture, framed by our hut's large window, was another demonstration of the forces being witnessed.

And it was during this period that what lived in, or depended on, the sea added another dimension to its fascination for me – the thousands of penguins and other birds, elephant, weddell and other seals and (only too rarely seen) whales, all depending on this watery home for food and movement. Watching the penguins shooting like bullets high out of the water to land on the pack ice before waddling, often miles, back to their nest site of the previous years; seeing leopard seals lurking offshore to hunt these very same penguins – such sights added to the lure of the sea itself.

But all this could be witnessed from the shore or a boat – even more fascinating was the first glimpse of the world that existed under the surface. Diving became a routine programme at the Base and it soon offered an opportunity for novices like me to venture into this watery world as a learner. In those days, an ill-fitting secondhand wet suit was a poor barrier to the cold, even starting with a kettle of hot water poured between skin and rubber. To view the living underwater system close up was a revelation.

Only much later, after having moved to Cromarty, did the opportunity arise to become a qualified diver, by this time living in a house overlooking the Cromarty Firth. With my job also transferring from Antarctic science to conservation in the Highlands, I was in the perfect position to feed my obsession – to look out on the sea over breakfast, to deal with marine and coastal conservation around one of Britain's most important coastlines, to dinghy sail or occasionally cruise on its surface or to explore its underwater secrets with the Inverness divers.

Memorable wildlife spectacles have been innumerable: our own local dolphins, seals and otters never cease to captivate; the annual pilgrimage of thousands of ducks and geese; wheeling flocks of glittering waders; gannets plunging for food off St Kilda; huge rafts of guillemots on the sea surface near their high rise accommodation; or the huge seabird breeding colonies themselves, all around our coasts.

But equally breathtaking for me have been the close range encounters with animals whilst diving. The variety of form and colour which suddenly springs to life as the torch beam hits them is truly amazing – a complex community of organisms, clinging to rock faces, emerging from sand or shingle or gliding around in the water. There is an immediate wish to share these wonders with others. If only people knew what was down there they'd be more concerned to protect it.

Then there's the hypnotic music of waves lapping the shore. Whether experienced while going to sleep in a tent or hut abroad, or beachcombing on the Black Isle, it never fails to calm the soul.

Nearly thirty-two years have now passed since arriving in Cromarty and although the sailing and diving have unfortunately ceased, the passion for my daily fix of sea watching is as strong as ever. Having also looked underwater briefly in several other parts of the world, I'm even more conscious that the marine life in the seas around Scotland is almost as interesting. We have a wonderland on our doorstep.

Just as with the situation on land, though, I frequently get depressed at how we humans have ill-treated the sea's complex web of life. Now that we know so much more about how interdependent all its inhabitants are, and how dependent we are on them, it is so frustrating to see this still being ignored. Restoration of the health of the sea and its potential natural biodiversity would be to everyone's benefit, but short-term imperatives seem to blind us to what action is required.

My direct involvement with marine conservation is now through voluntary work with the Scottish Wildlife Trust and Moray Firth Partnership, but even when that ceases, I know that my bond with the sea, that beguiling watery world that hides most of its treasures from our daily view, will not diminish.

Living by the sea

Sometimes I cycle by the sea,
I smell the fresh air and watch the dolphins jump with me,
Seagulls are squawking making their sound,
As I walk on rocky ground.

Looking in rock pool is always fun,
But not as lying peacefully in the sun,

Crabs walk sideways on the silky sand,
As the local town plays the band.

Walking by the sea,
Is what means the most to me.

By Zoë

It Certainly Beats the Chimney Pots

by John Talloch

7¹/₂ years in Cromarty

When I was small, living in the Kyles of Bute, the sea was a positive and comforting factor in our upbringing. We sometimes sailed down from Glasgow on the *Jeanie Deans,* one of the last paddle steamers. I remember being taken down into the engine room and watching in awe as these huge gleaming pistons pumped up and down. I remember also the neighbour who said, trying unsuccessfully to conceal her pride, "Ma John has got a job on the boats. He's to get twa pound and ten shilling a week. But, ach, we'll just live like ordinary folk just the same!"

When we moved to Stornoway in 1952 the sea, in the form of the Minch, became a more challenging proposition.

Since coming to Cromarty from Aberdeen in 1999, I have found both these aspects of the sea here. Looking towards Ben Wyvis in the evening, with the sun going down, the sea comes alive with red and pink and gold. But then I remember the monument down on the Links, with the powerful words of Hugh Miller describing the departure of Highlanders who had been torn from their homes and launched out on an uncertain future. For them, the sea around Cromarty must have represented the threat of the unknown.

For me, though, sitting in my study and looking out on the Cromarty Firth, I find the sea therapeutic. It certainly beats the chimney pots which I stared at for twenty years through the velux windows of my study at the top of the manse in Aberdeen.

Hugh Miller's moving inscription on the Emigration Stone reads: 'The Cleopatra as she swept past the town of Cromarty was greeted with three cheers by crowds of the inhabitants and the emigrants returned the salute, but mingled with the dash of the waves and the murmurs of the breeze their faint huzzas seemed rather sounds of wailing and lamentation than of a congratulatory farewell.'
Photo by May Hunter.

Walking with Hugh

by Martin Gostwick

Manager, Hugh Miller Museum

Whenever I walk the shores of Cromarty, I cannot help seeing them through the eyes of Hugh Miller, having become immersed in his sea stories almost as soon as my wife Frieda and I arrived here fifteen years ago to look after his museum.

And I thrill to see how our young people enjoy many of the same adventures as did the boy daredevil Hugh. I wish I too had been born here, and spent my youth delving the caves and ravines, taking a birl through the woods, and going for a swim and sail and fish in these waters in their wondrous setting.

I see Hugh, guided by his Uncle Sandy, scrambling over the pebbles on the ebb tide, spotting garnets, learning to recognise and name the cuttle fish, limpets, sea-mice, crabs and couries. I see him trapped in the Doocot Cave with his friend Findlay and getting a cheer at school for his doggerel verse about it.

Young Kieran from our neighbours sometimes brings gleaming mackerel to our door, fresh-caught same as Hugh landing his supper off the Sutors with wife Lydia in his yawl in the 1830s.

It is such a delight when fossil-hunters young and old bring in to the museum their own finds of scraps of ammonites and belemnites in the Cromarty deposits. Occasionally they have fragments of those extraordinary black-scaled Devonian creatures which Hugh carried back to the very same building and made world-famous 170-odd years ago.

Hugh's legends dramatise any stroll through today's quiet Cromarty. I cannot pass 'The Retreat' in Church Street without thinking of that awful smuggler tale in which a father accidentally kills his own son during a brawl with customs officers. Out at sea, there could be old salmon fisher Hossack on his way to barter his catch for gin from the noble smuggler Lord Byron (the poet's half-mad, rogue uncle).

Now and again a minke pays a call, minding you of the whale once hooked on "Nanny Fizzle's crook," which eventually beached in the Beauly Firth.

Then, on the way to 'The Hundred Steps', I see Captain Reid vanquishing the mermaid to win the hand of his sweetheart. Look out to sea again, and there see the herring shoals which once "lumped" in a solid silver drove from shore to shore.

Many are Hugh's tales of shipwreck in the days of sail, including of course that of his own father, and these legends too bear dramatic witness to the ever-present menace of storm we can see for ourselves to this day, though we are no longer exposed to the same dangers.

Hugh gives us history as well as legend, inviting us to visualise the changes wrought by the march of time. As we walk on the still steadily eroding shore paths, we can try to imagine what the medieval burgh, now buried under the sands, looked like; and to envision the cornfields and clumps of wood which in the 17th century surrounded the Clach Malloch stone.

For me, heritage has to be a living force, illuminating our past, informing us while, today, we make new history as we go along, history which will fill out a picture for those who come after us. In this book, we continue a great tradition begun by Hugh Miller.

Martin Gostwick and Hugh Miller.   *Photo by Calum Davidson.*

Cromarty Boat Club

by George Selvester

The Cromarty Firth is an excellent harbour, like old Dan Defoe and the Urquhart mannie said. Of all the places on the east coast of Britain, I would say this is the ideal place to have a yacht club. The Moray Sail Training come over from Lossiemouth and spend a lot of time in this firth, bringing people up to yachtmaster and so forth. The waters are generally calm unless you have a 'fetch' from Invergordon. If you have a strong westerly or north-westerly it can be uncomfortable but it is not downright dangerous. You can have short sharp waves which are not too difficult, although they do make a lot of people seasick, by the way.

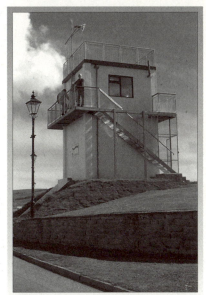

The restored Boat Club Tower.
Photo courtesy of George Selvester.

The old Cromarty yacht club fell away in 1963. When I came here it was totally defunct. I joined the Chanonry Club at Fortrose but they were more interested in promoting dinghy sailing, so after a year I joined the Invergordon Boat Club, a great bunch of guys who have a very enthusiastic racing programme for the bigger boats, 26ft and above, out-and-out racing machines. The answer, it seemed to me, was to start another boat club at this end of the firth to cater for more affordable sailing, looking after owners of craft such as my own. In late 1995 I sent a letter to the local newspapers asking for anyone with an interest in forming a club at Cromarty to attend a public meeting. The response was overwhelming – over fifty people attended the meeting and a steering committee was formed.

In April of 1996 Cromarty Boat Club was formally constituted and a full committee elected. The Flag Officers of the first committee were myself as Commodore, Bill Fraser (Dolphin Ecosse) as Vice Commodore, Alex Davidson as Secretary and Ronald Young (Cromarty Ferry Skipper) as Treasurer.

Alex then started to act as crew on my boat *Fat Sam* and soon we would have the first organised races and re-introduced the popular Cromarty Regatta. The problem we had, though, was no proper premises, either for over-wintering the boats, or a clubhouse. The hard by the pier and the ruinous observation tower were obviously suitable locations.

Cromarty 2000, a company set up for the refurbishment of the whole harbour area, expressed delight at the forming of a boat club, which they believed would strengthen their case. It was extremely unfortunate that their project failed at the last funding hurdle, but we still had an opportunity.

We obtained a tentative verbal agreement for a lease on the tower with the Laird Michael Nightingale, and were on the point of sending off the first cheques when he sadly passed away and the whole idea was shelved. But Alex and I continued to discuss all the possibilities. The committee approached Michael's son, John, to try to negotiate leasing the land around the harbour (which until now had been nothing but an eyesore) as well as the tower. Right from the very start John Nightingale was extremely helpful and in a relatively short time we had lease agreements on both the boat park project and the tower. The leases both came into effect on January 1st 2001, the boat park for a period of ten years and the tower for twenty-five years.

We realised that we could only tackle one problem at a time so went for the easier of the two to start with, and that was the boat park. After negotiating successfully with the Community Council over the plans, we soon got planning permission.

The problem now was where to get the money! Alex made the raising of the necessary funding look like a cakewalk. The total amount required for the project was £8,000 and our principal funders were Ross and Cromarty Enterprise (RACE) who gave around £5,000 and the Moray Firth Partnership £1,000. Alex also dealt superbly with all the administration, even down to organising the contractors. I directed the building contractors to the levelling of the compound and the fencing contractors as to the position and dimensions of posts, gates etc. The boat park was open, ready for use, by the end of the 2001 season.

We felt that the tower would be a more difficult nut to crack. The basement is a First World War-built structure, certainly bombproof at the time. Its walls are 3ft thick and may have provided a generator room for the company that was on the Links. During the Second World War the top part of two storeys was added, one of several round the firths from which the practices for the D-Day landings were monitored.

In the 1990s it was derelict, a broken-glassed, dark-stained, paint-peeling eyesore, just like everything else round there, detracting enormously from the appeal of the old harbour and that end of the Links.

We initially invited professionals to advise us, but found ourselves being proposed a grandiose monument rather than a useful building. After a lot of discussion the committee agreed that we act as our own agents in the project. We felt we had bitten off more than we could chew at times, but fortunately the opening of the boat park had started to swell our membership and all sorts of previously unsuspected talents emerged. Charlie Bateman and others revealed their knowledge of building and planning, drawing and general construction. Bill Fraser, a retired architect living in Cromarty, was a huge help in designing. Gavin Meldrum drew up lists of necessary tasks and allotted these tasks to the person most able to do them. Alex had to stay away from contractors, and me from funders, in case I upset them. Imagine!

By the end of the 2002 season we were in a very favourable position on all fronts except funding. Contracts were sent out to tender and wherever possible we asked local tradesmen to quote for all the work. Then in 2003 we were knocked back on all our funding applications, every one. One of the problems was a failure to show financial benefit to the wider community. Undaunted, Alex then did research, wrote a business plan and a brilliant presentation showing that the facilities for members and especially, visiting boat-owners, our toilet, showers and washer/dryer etc, were going to bring at least £16,000 a year into Cromarty.

At last, after several more frustrating failures Alex came through with the news that it was all systems go! The whole project was costed at

£33,477.16. The principal funders for this project were the Community European Development programme (CED) £16,000. For this amount we had to have match funding. This came from Ross & Cromarty Enterprise (RACE) £15,000 and Highland Council £1,000. The remaining £1,477.16 was from club funds.

Work started during March 2003 and to start with seemed to take forever to get off the ground as we continually hit little niggling problems that set us back by several days. We had already decided upon an opening day, 5th May. I proved adept again at getting upset and then upsetting others. Gavin Meldrum made me step back and chill out for a couple of days. We opened on deadline.

It was very gratifying that 90% of the membership did a little bit of work or donated items for the running of the new clubhouse. In many cases we had members who donated items and worked on the decorating and landscaping.

I think that the project brought us all together so that we gelled into a club at last. I have to thank every one of them from the bottom of my heart! Especially Alex Davidson, who has now returned to his home country, Canada.

Since then, the Aberdeen University marine biology team have taken over the old British Legion hut and grounds, and they too have been superbly smartened up. The harbour area is now a well-ordered, visually appealing and serene attraction to visitors in its own right.

We have a full write-up in the Reeds Almanac annually which will ensure our name goes everywhere there are keen sailors. We have a very functional clubhouse with tremendous facilities for the visiting yachtsmen who have now started to arrive from all over Britain and Europe. When the club was founded we had eight boats in an unkempt hard. The park now has 21 spaces, 30ft x 10ft wide. It is full, and we are about to expand to accommodate up to 30 boats. 2007 will see our eleventh season, and we will be among the proud hosts for the visit of the traditional boat flotilla which will berth here as part of the Year of Highland Culture.

~~The sea~~ The sea the sea has so many creatures above and below.

Above it has people in boats and seagulls in the air. Below it has big whales, little fish and squdgy squids.

Calum

At the beach

Living by the Sea is fun
When there is lots of Shining Sun
Paddling Splashing getting Wet
you could even take your pet.

You can make castles in the Sand
maybe even use your hand
get Some Shells or make a moat
Or maybe make a Smashing boat.

The ferry gives you a lovely ride
Over to the Other Side
When we get home we had Such
fun playing in the lovely Sun.

by Amy

Gladys Shepherd, swimming costume at the ready.
Photo by Calum Davidson.

Gladys Shepherd, nèe Parsley, was born in Hull in 1939 and moved to Cromarty with her family in 1952 when her father took up post as Coastguard. Apart from three years living and working in London after leaving school, and a few months in the USA in 1983, Gladys has lived in Cromarty ever since.

We used to live in Hull and often went across the Humber to Cleethorpes, which was lovely. The tide went out for miles and miles and the ferries there were huge car ferries. We came to Cromarty in 1952, travelling to Invergordon by train. And when we got there they said we had to get the ferry to Cromarty. There were six children and my Mum and Dad, so there was quite a pile of us. And we got to the harbour and my Mum said to the harbour master "Is the ferry for Cromarty coming, or is it here?" "Oh", he said "there's it out in the sea", and you could see it going up and down like this and my Mum said "I'm not going on that coggie boat". (*Coggie* meant a little rowing boat, not a ferry as such.) My mother couldn't envisage a ferry being such a little boat.

But we did go on it, and Albert used to go across to Invergordon three times a day and he would bring the papers and the mail and the supplies and he used to take all the rabbits from Cromarty that used to go to Hull on the freight train from Invergordon. It's funny, we used to go into the city (Hull) on a Saturday morning to the markets to get the fish and the rabbits and everything that came from Scotland and we'd buy rabbit because it was a Sunday lunch for us: it was a treat, we loved it. And here were piles and piles of boxes down by the harbour in Cromarty to go over to Invergordon. That was so amazing! And I remember going up to Davidston and all the rabbits were running wild and we thought we could catch them, there was that many of them. I don't know who used to kill them and freight them but they were all piled up. There used to be Jock the trapper, he would have been the one. He lived in Allan Square.

We used to go over the ferry and my Mum would say: "Oh you're not wise, you want your brains washing out, going on that ferry". It would be disappearing in the waves, but we used to go and get our hair done in Invergordon and I got my ears pierced over there and my father went mad, but I mean it was all across water and it was lovely.

The *Eagle* and the *Ark Royal* used to come into the firth regularly when I was young. They'd anchor off Cromarty on a Sunday and we used to go out and get a guided tour and they would feed us: beautiful food all laid out – salmons and that. Catriona Gillies, Maggie Reid, all that age group, used to go at night – to big buffets and things, you know, the officers used to entertain them all – they had a wonderful time. We used to love going out to the big ships.

The sailors would come into Cromarty – the dances we had with the sailors, oh, there were dances every Saturday night. The local boys used to get mad: there was always a punch up because the girls were dancing with all the sailors! We used to have some fun. The sea was a big thing then.

Like the rigs nowadays the ships would come in here for service because it's a deep port. They would anchor just off Cromarty and we loved it when they came in. And then of course there was the *Prince Louis,* with the boys from Gordonstoun. It anchored off Cromarty and the boys would come in, in the little rowing boats, and the girls would all be waving. I was about 13 or 14. And we'd be standing in the classroom looking out to sea. "Oh, the *Prince Louis* has come in", we'd say, and it was a Mr Mackenzie who was our teacher then. "If you'd like to stand, girls, you can stand for the rest of the day, but in the corner", he'd warn. But you couldn't see out of the window then.

And then of course my Dad was the Coastguard and if it was more than 5 or 7 force gales the cone would go up and he would go up to a lookout at the top of the Sutors – they would look out for SOS signals and all that, doing about a four-hour watch and then the next one would go up. My Dad had one of those motorised bikes with an engine on it. We used to go up with him sometimes and just stand and watch what he did. He'd keep a log of things that were happening in the water and boats that were coming in. The lookout has been pulled down now, I think, but the sheds are still there. People used to live in them, looking after the pigs that were owned by Colonel Ross.

The first year we came, at the first Regatta, there were all the races: swimming across the harbour basin, relay swimming race, the greasy pole and things, and my sister and I entered for the races with swimming caps and we were the only ones there – nobody else went in! Even my ex husband couldn't swim and he'd lived in Cromarty all his life. They used to jump off the shed in the Vee, you know, down the harbour; we used to all go swimming there and it would be choc-a-block with young ones learning to swim, and then there were quite a few came up that were getting lessons and we were all swimming then. The Regattas were good. Eventually some older ones used to go in for the 'greasy pole': they would hang a salmon on the end and if you got to the end of the pole, you got the salmon! It was really good fun.

We used to go out on the sewage pipes, you know, and swim! When you think about it now…but I kept my mouth well shut! I suppose it never did us any harm. If we saw anything nasty, we'd move away from it. I remember walking out on the sewage pipes, they were quite slippery. We'd go on them when the tide was out, to see what we could see on the beach. Also we used to go and collect mussels. A lot of people collected mussels and winkles as we called them. They don't call them that here.

We had a local fisherman, Big Robert, Jimmy Mallaig's brother. He had his own little boat and he used to go out fishing twice a week and he had a push barrow and would go round selling this fish. My Mum used to buy the fresh fish and my Dad would do it on the fire with batter on it. Fish was a big thing then. They used to catch everything:

cod, haddock, flatfish, occasionally crabs and lobsters. Every Friday we got our fish, you know, everybody ate fish on a Friday.

Of course my son-in-law, Bob Maclean, has swum to Nigg, was it two or three years ago, and Pete Clunas and Fraser Mackenzie. I've never swum to Nigg but my sister June might have done. I was always quite frightened of the deep water and I hated seaweed round your legs and the thought of an eel round your leg, ugh! I mean, I love looking at the sea and I love walking on the beach. I do love swimming, but I prefer to go to a pool than in the sea. Mrs Middleton of Rose Farm used to go in the sea a lot. She had her own steps and her own caravan. She was marvellous.

We used to go to Nigg for Sunday School sausage sizzles. Even when I was married and had children we used to go across to Nigg for a treat. We would take a picnic and then go to the hotel for soft drinks and lollipops for the bairns. The beach was absolutely beautiful. It's still there (to the east) but I mean the sand was the whole way along and right round the bay. It was just like being abroad, you know, I mean it was famous – just like a holiday resort. We used to pray for good weather and get ready on the Sunday. We'd put the bairns to Sunday school and then when they came back we'd get their costumes and everything and over we went. They'd be in and out of the sea all day. We didn't come home till late. The boat used to go back and fore, I think it was about a shilling (10p) in those days.

The lifeboat used to take people out on trips quite a lot. They used to charge pennies and take you right out the Sutors and there was an RAF one from Invergordon: I think it was a pilot boat for the big boats coming in, and it took you right out the Sutors as well. And there were loads and loads of yachters used to come to the hotel on a Sunday with their boats, from Invergordon, Saltburn and all around that coast and from Findhorn. Every Sunday they'd come to the hotel for their lunch and they would have the presentations of the prizes for the races in the hotel. All this was in the 50s and 60s. All the boats would come in – Cromarty was great and there were more shops then. But it's nice to see yachts actually *from* Cromarty in the bay now. When they're out in the summer, it's lovely.

When I lived in Bayview Crescent you'd get up in the morning and you'd see all the 'tumblers' as we used to call them. Probably it was dolphins, I don't know, perhaps porpoises: millions of them, they used to be in their droves. There was never a day that you didn't see them. They'd be jumping right out the water, beautiful. I used to love that. And you could see Ben Wyvis from across the water – in fact, my relations used to come up from England and they'd say "it's like a 5-star hotel here", you know, the view. You don't appreciate it when it's on your doorstep. I appreciate it more because I have no view here (in the Hugh Miller Institute flat). I've been here over 20 years now. But you can't see the sea from here, which is a shame.

Betty Hogg and some of us used to go in the sea every summer, just from the beach. There was loads of us used to go in from the beach. It was a regular thing. You'd hear "Are you coming? Get your cozzie on!" I remember a day quite recently when Doris (McCann) said to me "Would you like to go for a swim?" I said, "I'd love to go" (thinking she was going to Dingwall baths). I said, "I'll get my cozzie on" because it's quicker when you get there. And then she stopped down the road and took out a flask. And she makes beautiful muffins and here we were on the beach! It was *freezing*. She put her toe in, I put my toe in and "Och, to heck", I said and I got in and she said, "You're brave", and then she came in and we were in and out for ages and it was lovely. Jellyfish? I didn't see any. There used to be, when we were young – used to be millions in the Vee. It used to bother me a bit, swimming amongst them – I didn't like it. I've never been stung with one but a few people were. And then standing on them on the beach sometimes! I saw the crabs and things, you know, and I used to think you'd get your toe pinched.

I remember being interviewed for television, asking about the oil rigs and what difference it had made to our lives, the rigs being in Cromarty, and I said it did make a big difference to money. But the men just went mad with it; I mean it didn't really benefit the families. My ex husband and all his family and his friends got huge pay packets but the wives never saw half of it. I said on that interview, it made a difference because we got £6 a week when he worked for Colonel Ross on the farm, and he gave me £50 when he went to Nigg, which was big money. But they were getting about £150-£200 a week or more and he gave me £50 and that was for all the children and everything, you know. The standard of living did improve, although I spent every penny on my children, food and the house.

I used to love picking up shells, you know, pretty shells, when we were young and we used to make necklaces and things. When we were very young we were always at the seaside, I always associated the seaside with rock and humbugs and fish and chips.

I don't think the young folk feel quite the same way about the sea – there are too many computers, too many other things. My grandsons love sport: golf and things, and they go to the gym. They don't seem to use the sea like we did.

Cromarty Sea Change

by Archie Mactaggart

It was something of a shock to be informed that the area just outside our house had been chosen as the site for the new sewage pumping station. Since 2004 this site has handled – if that is the proper word – the bulk of the raw sewage load from the town and pumps it out to the treatment plant at the Targets.

When the project was carried out we were more than a little dismayed because the plans provided by the Council were as usual indecipherable and incomplete. The final structure was significantly different, I think, from the paperwork.

Yet despite our misgivings the improvement to the shoreline of the whole town has been remarkable. No longer is there any evidence apart from normal flotsam of any of the ghastly detritus of modern sewage to be found on the shore, while the water quality has improved out of all recognition. How do I know that? For the last two years the number of migratory sea ducks which used to visit the old pipe on the beach daily to feed in the wintertime have almost disappeared, with only the odd merganser now showing up occasionally.

The Harbour – recently dredged – seems to be much cleaner and although debris from the Inner Firth still makes an occasional appearance, the whole Cromarty shoreline has been vastly improved. When winds come from the right direction the beach at the Links fills up with lovely clean white sand and everyone, especially visitors, enjoy what is a considerable local amenity.

Cromarty is of course renowned for its character as a town, and lately I myself have heard visitors remarking on how nice that "little cottage" at the foot of the Sutor looks. Sometimes I tell them, sometimes I don't. So full marks to the originator of that design of sewage treatment plant.

By contrast, I remember being told by one of the workmen – when I enquired about landscaping the pumping station as the job drew to a close – that the gaffer was as we spoke working out a landscaping scheme, to all intents and purposes on the back of an envelope. The Community Council thoughtfully and thankfully took that particular duty from him.

The Sewage Project would – given the lack of controversy attaching to it – seem to be a great success and a good modern amenity for the future of the town.

As this is a personal view of the development, I would mention the contractors who built the pumping station. This work was carried out by a small, dedicated team of men from Perth whose professionalism and focus did great credit to them all. They carried out all their work with considerable consideration for the locals most affected by the necessary disturbance.

A View from Clunes

by Jill Campbell

19 years in Cromarty

The sea – cold, wet, salty. But not as mucky as it was pre-sewage plant. Beachcombing is nicer without the 'thingies'. No more does the sea gurgle and slurp beneath the big slab in my garden. Those old pipes connect to the new pump.

The sounds of the sea whispering and roaring and its colours are uncountable. I wish I'd kept a diary for the last 19 years. A sea diary, I mean.

Textures, too. Silk – yes. Oily, inky. But did you see it that day when it was a giant bar-code? Must have started smooth. Then a breeze combed across the whole lot. And then was it streaked with a fork?

Going to the seaside was a treat years ago. But why? Many reasons, but the one I prefer just now is my sense of its largeness and its amiability. Irrational? Yet to a small child on sunny sands, that benign, salty wetness is safe. Only the wasps and the adults spoil things.

And now? Obviously the sea is far from being a friend. A companion it is, though: has moods, a huge wardrobe, a capacity to delight, to alarm and its own musical conversation. It offers food too. If only it could also cook.

Living by the Sea

Living by the sea is fun but sometimes it can be a bit dangerous because if someone could fall off the harbour they could drown. I think this is some of the fun things to do fishing, swimming, going on boats to see the sea creatures and paddling to see if you can get some hermit crabs. I think that the harbour is going to fall down in 2 to 3 years. So if anybody is on the Cromarty harbour so be careful.

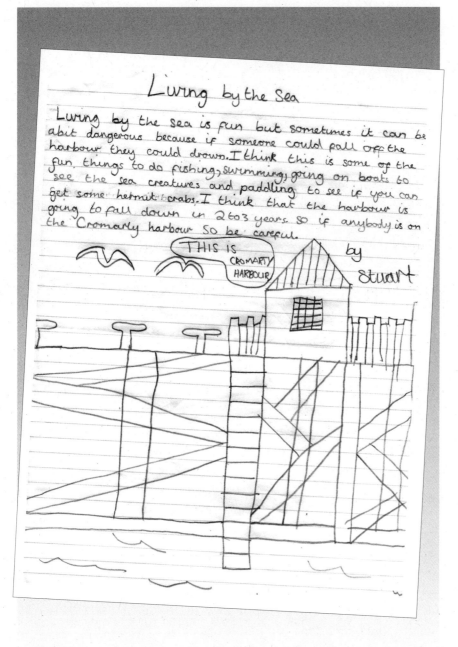

THIS IS CROMARTY HARBOUR

by Stuart

Hamish Gunn with family in Bonxie, the boat he built when aged 10.
Photo courtesy of the Gunn family

Born in Shetland, Hamish Gunn was five when his family moved to Cromarty in 1982. He left Fortrose Academy at 16 to attend Glasgow's Nautical College, after which he worked first in the Merchant Navy and currently with a private company, Blue Water, as Lead Maintenance Technician and nightshift supervisor on board an FPSO in the North Sea.

In Cromarty the sea was all you did – it's all there was. I mean, we didn't spend an awful lot of time at home – it's not like now with PlayStations. We were never at home, me and the boys. If we weren't in the woods or up at the Forts, we were down on the beach or down at the harbour. But Dad had a strict thing about the harbour: we weren't allowed there unattended until we could prove that we could swim. So Dad had the 'Harbour Test': we had to swim from the end of the harbour to the beach at high tide. Then he was happy that we were safe. But I couldn't swim. All my pals would be down the harbour and I'd be really upset. Then I went away to Brittany on holiday and learnt how to swim while there. The day I got home, I said "Right, Dad, that's it, down the harbour now" and did my swimming test. I must have been about eight.

In the summer we lived in the harbour – we didn't do anything else. We were down there first thing in the morning. We'd have all our stuff for taking crabs out of the water, for shellfish, everything. All we'd do was just swim, all day. We'd get bits and bobs to eat there, from the shops if we had to, but most of the time we just lived down there, went home at night. Everyone just hung around there, maybe about a dozen of us, all summer, jumping off the harbour. It would have to be pretty dire for us not to be down there.

I remember we went out one time, me and the other guys, and the weather was horrific, appalling, the wind and the swell were really serious. It was actually painful to stand on the sand because the wind was ripping the sand. We thought it'd be good fun in the big waves but the tide was going out and we'd do silly things like jump into the current – we knew that if you drifted out with the current it'd take you out past the harbour and you'd just swim off the side and go to the slipway, where the Ferry comes in. But that particular day the waves were so big you couldn't swim at all and I can remember a couple of us were clinging on under the bridge and a couple of the old fellers who always sat on the bench threw the rings down and pulled us up. I always remember the scrape of the barnacles. But that wasn't the worst of it – it was the hard time we got off them, you know! Rapped round the lug! They sent us home to our parents, leaving us in no doubt that they would know about it. I was scared at the time but it didn't stop us going back in, just not when the weather was so bad. That was the scariest experience I had down the harbour.

I remember there were a couple of summers, really good spells, and we were getting the Avoch fishing boats coming in during the night. They'd ditch an awful lot of stuff in the harbour at night, including octopus which we never got before. We used to catch them regularly. We'd also be pulling a lot of edible crabs out of the water and there was a gas kettle and we were cooking them up and flogging them to the tourists.

It's funny, as you go round the coast, everybody calls crabs different names. In Cromarty I would call an edible crab a 'kai' and the small green ones you see washed up on the shore a 'parton'. But if you go further up the coast, up to Balintore, where my wife's family's from, they call edible crabs 'partons'.

We'd be down with masks and snorkels as soon as it was low enough to get in and out of the piles, pulling crabs out. You'd get dinner-plate sized crabs: monsters, cracking-sized crabs in the harbour. You've got those piles that were added on during World War I. But you've also got the original stone walls with blocks missing and it's just a haven for lobsters and that sort of thing. Lobsters were a lot harder to catch than crabs because if you stuck your hand in a hole and grabbed a claw, they'd just shed it and disappear. And every now and again you'd look in and there'd be a conger eel. But everybody was always ready for them. I mean we went down with stuff for snorkelling and part of your gear would be a couple of baited hooks in case a conger eel appeared. And it'd be about a two-hour job to try to catch them because you have to coax it out with a fish on a big hook and then you'd have a trebler (a three-pronged big hook) to rip it up on a wire trace – some of them were 6' long and you'd be dragging them over the piles to get them out and then kill them. And half of it would go to The Royal Hotel and the other half would go home. They were absolutely beautiful to eat – incredibly bony but beautiful white meat, really nice. We used to catch all sorts. And then in the evenings we'd be round by the sandbanks, fishing for lugworm or what have you. At the lowest tides of the year you'd get amazing crabs out at the 'Clach Malloch' rock. It was always a big thing to go out there – it's quite far out.

When I was ten I built a boat. My Christmas and birthday present that year was three sheets of marine ply! I built a wee, eight ft pram dinghy and called it the *Bonxie;* it was a good boat, built to a design from one of Dad's 'Classic Boat' magazines. And of course we were always on the sea because Dad had a boat – we were always out with him, first of all a Shetland rowing boat with a bow at each end, but then a clinker-built gaff rig with red sails, a beautiful boat with two masts which was quite a hard boat to sail. When my uncle went to the States in the mid 80s he sold Dad his boat: a fibreglass hull, just a breeze; anybody could sail it on their own.

I used to go out on my own in the *Bonxie.* Dad's rule was that you had a lifejacket on at all times, and that was it, he didn't mind – he knew we could all swim. We never went as far as Nigg in it – it was only a rowing boat – but we did get shouted at from some of the rigs. We'd be trying to get in under the pontoons and were sworn at from above! When we sailed with Dad he would tow the *Bonxie* behind and we'd go over to Nigg, moor, and then row in.

It was really good at Fortrose Academy because at that time they had Sandy Mackenzie ('Laddy'). He was a brilliant teacher who taught seamanship which, for the likes of the Avochie lads who were at the fishing, was fantastic for them. 'Laddy' was ex merchant navy and when they had the Friday afternoon 'Leisure Activities', Sandy would run boat-building during the winter (when we made two Mirror dinghies) and then during the summer we'd sail them down at Fortrose harbour. For a summer I was in the Chanonry Sailing Club at Fortrose. It was great to learn to sail properly but I'm not the slightest bit competitive, I just liked to go and do it for fun.

I think I always knew I wanted to be at sea. I thought about the Royal Navy to start with but after going for all the tests I thought it was very 'controlling', very strict. I don't think I'd have lasted two minutes! I knew Robert Hogg and Donald Beauly and Donald's sister Hermione – they all went into the Merchant Navy. And then a friend of Dad's told us about Clyde Marine and took us down for an interview because by then I had left school. I was 16 when I went to the Nautical College in Glasgow for three years, sponsored through Clyde Marine. I had a year in College, a year at sea and then a final year at College. I was an engineer – we keep the thing running, keep the lights on.

I'm not Merchant Navy any more, I work offshore. I did a couple of years qualified and then I took a sideways slide onto an FPSO (a Floating Production and Storage Offloading unit): it's a ship that produces. The platforms that Ardersier and Nigg built are a thing of the past now. I mean, why build something that sits on the seabed for thirty years and then what do you do with it? For a fraction of the price you can convert a ship, float it on top of the well, let it produce, let it fill up with oil and every now and then a tanker comes alongside and you just pump the oil out into it and the tanker takes it away.

The one I was on before, the *Seillean,* was ex BP. *Seillean* is 'bumblebee' in Gaelic. Most FPSOs are moored; they go to where they are needed and they stay there. On the *Seillean* we weren't connected to the seabed. We were 'DP', i.e. 'dynamically positioned': we used satellites to hold us in position and we would float over the well and had our drill pipe riser which could connect us to the seabed. When the weather got bad or anything happened we could just disconnect in seconds. So this thing, when it was first designed for the North Sea, it would go to one well, fill up, go to another well, fill up and then go back to shore – like a bumblebee going round flowers. But then BP sold it and another company took it over and it was converted for deep water. And that's when I was working on it, down in Brazil. I was six years on it down there and it's still there.

The thing I'm on now is only the second FPSO ever made: the *Uisge gorm* which is Gaelic for 'Blue Water', which is the name of the company I work for. All their vessels are called Blue Water in different languages. It's in the same place all the time – about 200 miles east of Newcastle - just over an hour in a chopper from Aberdeen. I'm the senior/lead Maintenance Tech, managing and maintaining all of the machinery onboard, to supply power everywhere, keep the lights on and keep us producing. I'm on permanent nights but you get used to it. I absolutely love my job; it's just being away that's not good.

It's amazing that I don't have a boat. I want to get my kids on the sea, give them the opportunities I had. There's so much there. I've seen some pretty hairy things at sea and it is incredibly powerful, but everything in it is absolutely amazing. So many people don't realise, even down in Cromarty harbour, that there's so much wildlife there. People probably think there's a couple of crabs, a couple of shellfish under there, but really there's so much more. Cromarty harbour is fantastic.

Diving from the harbour – a traditional rite of passage. Photo by Calum Davidson.

Harbour Jumping

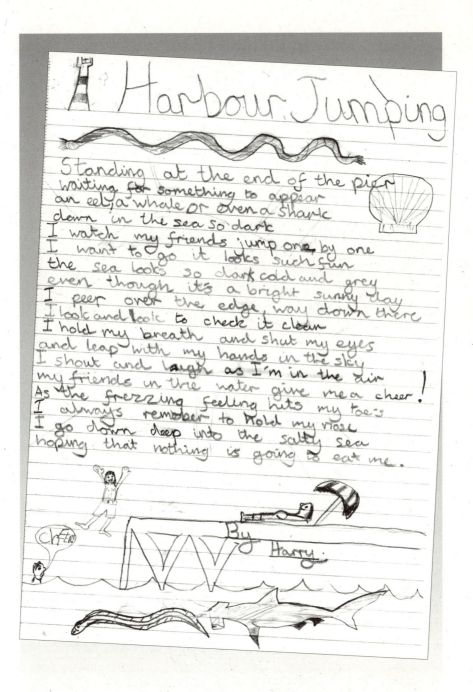

Standing at the end of the pier
waiting for something to appear
an eel, a whale or even a shark
down in the sea so dark
I watch my friends jump one by one
I want to go it looks such fun
the sea looks so dark cold and grey
even though it's a bright sunny day
I peer over the edge, way down there
I look and look to check it clear
I hold my breath and shut my eyes
and leap with my hands in the sky
I shout and laugh as I'm in the air!
my friends in the water give me a cheer!
As the freezing feeling hits my toes
I always remember to hold my nose
I go down deep into the salty sea
hoping that nothing is going to eat me.

CHEER!

By Harry.

101

Childhood Terrors

by Fran Tilbrook

31 years in Cromarty

I'm standing on the raised beach, idly watching a family of three small girls playing excitedly on the sandy shore. Barefoot, they run up and down to the distant waves, their long hair streaming behind them, their shouts and cries carried to me on the breeze.

Half close my eyes and I'm transported back more than fifty years. I'm on holiday in Donegal, Ireland, with my two elder sisters. We're on a chilly beach, the sea some way off as the tide is out. We're wearing bobbly nylon swimsuits that tie around the neck, our short hair parted down the middle, held back by two kirby grips. My sisters dance and prance, play hopscotch and race to the sea's edge and back, daring the waves to catch them. They're calling to me.

Rooted to the spot, shivering not just from the chilly wind, I'm scared stiff. I'm gazing at the many worm casts blocking my route. How can I join in the fun and games? How can I paddle and splash as I've longed to do all holiday, without treading on these repellent structures? For I'm convinced that each one contains a coiled up worm ready to do something terrible to me if I touch it with my bare feet. I'm frozen with fear and revulsion, aware that I'm being babyish, yet unable to conquer this irrational dread and join my sisters.

Then two people – possibly my parents – take my arms and fly me down towards the others, my feet retracted like an aircraft's wheels. The relief is palpable: the sand is smooth again beneath the water. I am paddling. For the moment I feel safe, though my earlier dread of the worm casts is soon replaced by fear of the seaweed swirling around my ankles and the prospect of sea creatures touching my toes.

I can smile now at my dimly remembered childhood terrors. Watching these carefree girls on the beach today I'm glad that my own children and now two of my grandchildren have had the privilege of living by the sea in Cromarty. For me, an urban child, the sea and the shore represented both mythical magic and unspeakable fears. For my family, however, it's a familiar environment – one that brings only confident pleasure, not irrational dread.

The Cromarty Girl

by Howard Hunter

written for his wife Carol, a Cromarty girl

As the sun goes down on the rim of the hill,
And the shadows are long, grim and grey,
A red-headed girl with a beautiful smile
Looks out from the edge of the bay.

She picks up her stick and walks on through the streets
That are narrow and icy and cold,
Past Hugh Miller's Cottage and down to the firth,
It's a sight that she loves to behold.

She walks further on across beaches and stone,
Where the caves are great gaps in the hill,
And the seagulls all gather and scream overhead
With voices all harsh, high and shrill.

She hikes up South Sutor and catches her breath
At the views that she sees down below,
And after a while she goes down through the woods
Where the ferns and wild flowers all grow.

She watches the ferry boat, battered and bruised
Chug its long weary way 'cross the bay,
The Cromarty Girl has returned to her roots,
And some day she'll come back to stay.

Susan Florence in the NTS Hugh Miller
Museum garden.
Photo by Calum Davidson.

Susan Florence, nèe Manson, was born in Cromarty 53 years ago. Much of her childhood was spent fishing on or by the sea. Most unusually, she was one of 20 female welders among the workforce of 5,000 at Highlands Fabricators Yard at Nigg, helping to build oil rigs.

It was December 1973 when I started at Nigg as a welder's helper. They were recruiting at the time, the money was good, everybody was working there. It was better than going to Inverness to work. I was then trained as a Lloyds-trained welder at the Hi-Fab training school.

After nine months as a welder's helper I thought 'I can do that'. You were with a welder all the time and it was 'submerged arc welding' I started off on. It's a big machine with a big coil of wire on the top and you'd a bucket at the back and a flux came down and actually covered the wire as it was melting and the pipe just went round automatically. And all you were doing was guiding the weld. So I hounded the GF (general foreman) at the time – Tudor Lewis – and after about three months of me stopping him every time I saw him, "Can I not do my welding tests?" eventually he just said "Right, we'll give you a go, we'll put you on to it" and I passed the test and I went on to stick welding – that's ordinary welding – and then on the 'MIG' welding (metal inert gas).

There's different types of welding, you see. With sub-arc welding you're just sitting watching a pipe all day – very boring after 8 or 10 hours. The MIG welding is a routine weld: it's a base before your 'stick' or your 'sub arc' goes on. Because when your two cans are coming together there's always a gap – you have to have a gap. And the MIG just bridged the gap, you know, it's just a base weld for the other weld to go on top. But most of the time it's back-gouged out anyway (taken out by what they called 'gouging'. It's a long carbon rod which ripped out the weld). It was supposed to be back-gouged but quite a lot of the time we burnt it out. We weren't supposed to, but we did.

I've still got the old 'procedures' here – for the Conoco Rig in 1982. Before you start to weld, the pipes have to be pre-heated and the minimum pre-heat temperature was 100° C. That was before you started welding, I mean…welding is a very, very hot job, it really is. That's why I don't like the cold now, I think!

One of Susan's welding 'procedures' from the 80's Conoco rig.
Courtesy of Susan Florence.

We females wore exactly the same things as the men: a T-shirt and a boiler suit. It depended on where you were and what you were doing. If you were gouging, you wore moleskins because that's actually ripping out hot metal, melted metal. You always had a moleskin jacket on, and that was really hot. Some of the procedures here, minimum heat 100° C, max 250°C. You had temp sticks which actually melted at the temperature. There were different colours, different gradings – I think orange was the hot one that melted at about 250°C. And once that melted, you stopped welding then. And you'd wait until the pipe cooled down. But some of them were a minimum of 130°C before you started. Aaahh, you've no idea, it's very hot work!

I remember one time – Oh, God it was embarrassing! I was in a can and our squad was down in the hole, you know, where the rig was actually built. Our squad was normally in the Fab shops 1, 2, or 3. But some of the time we were sent down the hole, once the rigs were getting nearer to finishing. I was inside one of the cans, in one of the big flotation legs, and I had to back-gouge a manhole cover overhead. Oh my Lord, I was 40ft in the air on this scaffolding, up there on my own, back-gouging, and my jacket couldn't have been tied at my neck properly and the red hot metal went down my neck. Aahhh, I just stripped off and there was men working down below. I didn't give a damn, you know, I was burning and stripping everything off and it just melted my T-shirt. I was lucky, I caught it before it went properly into the skin. But I just stripped off, but not everything went, you know! Anyway, it was a couple of Croms that was working down below, so it wasn't too bad. I knew who they were. They knew themselves they'd to keep well clear anyway, because the hot metal's flying everywhere, you know.

I remember another time when I stepped into mid air! We were in Shop 2 at the time, doing sub arc welding with what they called a plough. It would actually run on rails, it wasn't the big, big machines. You could walk about the shop with them; they were manual. There was a big hole in the centre. For some unknown reason I went and walked from one end of this plate to the other and walked into this hole and I fell 15 ft and just caught the H-beams on the way down. If I hadn't, I'd have been splattered! I hurt my shoulder and in fact I've still got a lump in my leg yet. What a clatter I got. I don't know what I was thinking about! I just climbed down after that. It was all up on frames so I climbed down the frame.

I got electrocuted a lot of the time. Oh it was dreadful. Some of the pipes weren't earthed properly or anything, you know, and you touched a machine and you touched the pipe they were on if you were actually welding inside the cans themselves, and you could be 10ft, 15 ft down inside a can, you know, and the heat was at least 100°C before you even started. It's like working inside an oven.

What was it like, being a woman there? You did get a bit of harassment, a couple of times, maybe, but the squad I was in was nearly all Croms anyway: Cromarty men, so they sort of looked after me anyway. But it made no difference if you were a woman or not. You still had to do your job. With being a welder, you couldn't get away with it. You had to do your Lloyds testing and your work was tested for you — nobody else could do it for you, so I mean the welders got tested, every new rig. You had to put 105% into it instead of 100%. Some of the boys came up from Glasgow or Newcastle, with all the ones all their lives in shipbuilding and that, and to have a woman welder — it just wasn't the done thing. So you basically had to prove yourself — that you could do it and you were as good as them, if not better. But 99% of the time, once they saw that you could do your job, you could do what they did, you were accepted, or at least I was. But this is going back into the 70s so we were breaking new territory. Nowadays you've got women welders just two a penny, women engineers and that, it's an acceptable part of the way the world is now. We all looked out for each other, it was good.

But the conditions were horrendous. They wouldn't get away with it now. The heat was absolutely atrocious. We were lying on scaffolding boards that were actually smouldering, they were that hot. The boxes that we were working in, in Shop 3, were maybe 4ft x 8ft – it was just coffins we were in and they were all pre-heated up to 100°C, 160°C, 180°C, before you even started welding and you were in this, it was just layers of boxes, and if you were working in the bottom box there'd be a man working in the top box, so you've got his heat on top of you and you've got air breathing equipment which was just taken off a manifold and you're breathing this in. We were 20 minutes in and 10 minutes out, I think that's what we were allowed.

And the orange juice! It started off all right. I mean we were on gallons of this orange juice but then they started diluting it that much, it was just practically water we were getting. And we were on salt tablets as well – we had to go to the nurse to get salt tablets. The conditions were absolutely horrendous, they really were. And we weren't getting any more money for it – we were getting the same money as the fabricators and the riggers and it was totally wrong. So we went on strike. The general foremen were having nervous breakdowns – too much pressure, you see, to get the job done. They were taking it out on the foremen and the foremen were taking it out on us and six weeks I think we were out on strike before we got a decent wage for that job sorted out, and decent orange juice.

Thirteen years I was there. It was all right, it was an experience, but we never felt we were making history – it was just a job. And even when the rigs were floated out, I just thought 'Thank God I'm no working on that any more'. The welds we did will last, though they'll probably have to touch them up. Before the rigs went out we went down and scrawled our names everywhere in the cans. If a rig came in now that I actually worked on, I could tell what weld I did because I find it impossible to keep a straight line. I cannot even draw a straight line freehand. The start of my welds is like a dog's hind leg. The thing is, if your first weld isn't straight, then your second one's obviously not going to be straight to follow the first one, you know. My welds were always squint. You build the welds up. There are about 30 runs with a cap on top.

I wasn't sad to go. When I left, the camaraderie was already going down the hill. When we first started off we were part of a team, you know. And you weren't just a number, you were a name. But by the time the 80s came you were a number and as far as I know it's still the same to this day – you're expendable, they don't really care. I was there at the best time because it was new for everybody: the foremen, the GFs, were all from the farms, the forestry, or whatever; we were all in the same boat. I was quite glad to go, actually.

When I was at Nigg, I didn't like travelling on the bus if the boat wasn't running. I get travel sick. There were quite a lot of us that didn't like travelling on the bus. Well, at the end of backshift one October, November, time – it was quite dark, it was a really stormy night and the bus was on – the boat wasn't going to run. But somebody must have phoned the skipper of the *Coral Star*, John Patience, and he chanced it, taking back whoever was on the harbour at the time. We were all at the harbour and we thought 'Oh, he's never going to make it' but then he came and he didn't even get right into the harbour, we just jumped on to the boat and back he went…Oh…it was horrendous! I never really liked the *Coral Star* you know, there wasn't much keel on her and it didn't feel safe. I really thought I was going to meet my maker that night. And John was calling out "I canna hold her, she's going". How we didn't hit Davy Jones' locker, I'll never know. But he made it to the Cromarty side! And I'll always remember the first three people I saw on the pier: Jan Davie, Rob Davie, Alison. They thought the boat was going to go down.

And 'Buller' was on that night as well. He was holding on at the back to one of the guardrails that ran round the back of the boat. We couldn't believe it next day. The whole bar was bent. I mean, what strength to bend it, it was scaffolding tube, you know. You can't bend scaffolding tube! He must have been hanging on for dear life.

That crossing must have taken about 25 minutes. We normally did it in

8-10 minutes. That was about the only time I can say I was really, really scared in crossing. I think we all were. But it didn't put me off, the sea's in my blood. If we had gone over, one of the old fishers told me as a bairn: "If the boat ever goes down, take a deep breath and run for the shore"!

Childhood and pre-Nigg

In the summer time when we were bairns we used to go down and set lines: 50 houcks, 100 houcks, 200 houcks along at the Old Beddie, I mean you'd get a flukie (a flounder) and all along there. You don't take the 'Bigger Man'(a dab), they're horrible. We used to get mackerel and pollack in the Firth and we'd throw them away – they were just bait for the creels – we'd never eat them. And they cost a fortune now!

We'd go over to Nigg for bait. If not, we might get the bait down at the Old Beddie or we'd cycle out to Jemimaville and get bait there: lugworms. You just needed a grape there (a garden fork); you get lug all over the place. At the Beddies we'd use a lug spade. If not, we'd just go over to Nigg and get cockles and mushrooms. What we used to do was go and get Jimmy Mallaig's wee boat and row over to Nigg. I'd be about ten, eleven. I would never let my grandson cross the firth now. But then, it was nothing – we never thought anything of it. As long as you were home at night for your tea… I'm talking about Cromarty in the 60s you know. We were really the last of them – the ones with such freedom. That freedom just wasn't there in the 70s.

We made our own entertainment. We did a lot of fishing. I spent most of my time at sea. I used to go out with the salmon fishers. The first memory I have – I must have been about three or something like that and I was down at the salmon fishers. I was never away from the bothy, I was always in there. I was just fascinated by boats and the sea and everything.

They used to take me out and throw me up the bow; if not, I was sitting in the starn, you know. I can't swim to this day. No life jacket – never thought anything of it and yet you were stuck there and sitting on top of tarry rope. I love the smell of tarry rope to this day. And you just sat there and they were checking the leaders (the nets that guide the fish to the bag net.) The fish hit the leader and they just follow up the leader and they go into the bag net and they canna get out. The bag net was massive. They would check the leaders first for anything. You'd get cod or whatever stuck in them if they were big enough because the mesh was quite big. Then they'd take the ropes off the poles and check the bags. This was off the Blue Head, the Red Nose, MacFarquhar's Bed, Charlie's Seat, right out to the point of the Sutor there, but they went right up to Eathie.

The Ice House on the Links.
Photo by Fran Tilbrook.

And they used to take in some big fish, 30–40 lb salmon, you know. They'd take it in to the salmon bothy, then up to the Ice House. They were all thrown in the Ice House, cleaned and washed and everything. They were all packed in ice, packed in boxes and then off to the railway station in Inverness. I was involved in that all my childhood. I just loved going out in boats, you know. We used to go for our own kais (crabs) and lobsters when we were bairns. We'd go along the shore and always got a lobster at the Clach Malloch but only if you blocked up the holes – there's two or three holes for escape. You'd a cleek (a long bit of wire with a bend at the end) and you'd use that for kais and lobsters.

I mind one time when I was about eleven, twelve years old. It was a beautiful hot summer's afternoon and I was out fishing with Ali Maclean. The tide was just on the turn and we were over at the 'White Patch' (the bird cliffs on the North Sutor). I was facing the White Patch and Ali was facing Cromarty. He never said a word and when you're line fishing, you're just leaning over the side of the boat and your arm's just going back and fore and you're in a world of your own until you get a bite. And then this head just popped out of the water and said, "Hello!" Oh, I tell you, I nearly shed my skin, I was screaming. What a fright I got. And the skull cap! He had a skull cap on – it was John Robertson of Castlecraig. He was swimming quite a lot at the time, used to swim over to Nairn! He was just like a dolphin.

My husband built a boat and bought inkwell pots. Everybody knows the channel in the middle of the firth is quite deep, so we thought we'd drop the creels just on the edge of the channel there. Anyway we got 12 inkwell pots, it was quite a lot of money too to buy, you know. We put down 180ft of rope and I can't remember how many fathom on top of that again and we dropped the creels to the bottom and never seen them again! They were gone. 12 brand new pots and they were all strung together too, a quarter of a mile. It was so, so deep out there. And we had the sonar on board as well. We knew exactly where we were going. We could see we were on the edge of the shelf. But the current took them. I was quite peeved about that. Even if I got one dip out of them I'd have been quite happy.

I've never learnt to swim. I don't like going in the water. I like being on it, I've been on rafts, in canoes, in boats all my life. I was in the raft races before they made life jackets and all that compulsory. I don't think any of us on our raft could swim, and we were in the middle of the firth!

Years ago I tried to swim. My husband Mac does a lot of scuba diving – he's a seal – and I was determined I was going to conquer my fear of the water and he bought me a wetsuit. I was going to be really brave. I walked to the harbour in my wetsuit and flippers, down the slip and into where the pontoons are now and Mac was with me – he was in, swimming. "Right", he says, "in you go. Lie back on the water". "Oh my Lord," I says, my arms and legs sticking straight out to the side. That was fine, I was just starting to relax, when Mac took off! He went away and left me. Well, just as he went under the bridge and started swimming away, this wee tug came into the harbour and of course the wash came over me and as soon as it started going on my face and that, I just screamed blue murder. And the Legion was going at the time and I always mind, they all came out and they were all standing at the Legion door, looking and laughing. I mean, nobody attempted to rescue me or anything! Anyway, Mac eventually appeared and by this time I was hysterical. He stood me up in the water and do you know where the water was? Up to my knees. I was so embarrassed!

I love the sea, I love boats and everything, but I have never gone in the water since. If the Lord had meant me to be in the water, the Lord would've given me gills!

Fochabers and Cromarty

by Jess Matheson

I was born in Fochabers and although not living close by the sea we were always aware of it being not very far away – only a matter of a few miles as the crow flies. Fochabers nestles in a hollow, and so to enjoy the many beautiful walks surrounding it you have to climb to the higher ground and no matter what direction your walk takes you, be it through the forests or up on the moorland, you will always catch a glimpse of the Moray Firth in the distance.

Fish was a very valuable food source and we were fortunate to have two fishwives who called each week. They would arrive with huge creels on their backs, full to the brim with lovely fresh fish which they had carried for more than a mile from the railway station to the village. Fortunately they found a ready market with the village people and so their return journey was easier.

We had many outings to the seaside: Portgordon when we were very young children and Spey Bay when we were old enough to cycle there. I remember enjoying a wonderful holiday in Portgordon. Our temporary home was a bell tent and a whole new world opened up to us with the sea literally on our doorstep. Our 'camp site' was near the salmon fishers' nets and they used to keep us supplied with freshly caught flounders from the nets – delicious eating for hungry campers. We never needed to be entertained during our holiday by the sea; having sea, sand and rock pools was all that was necessary in those halcyon days.

I have lived by the sea for the past 30 years and have seen the sea in all its moods. One day it would be like a millpond with scarcely a ripple breaking the surface, the blue dome of the sky reflected on the glassy mirror below. Another time a strong wind would ruffle the surface, making the sea look angry and surly with the grey sky scowling above. But the full fury of the sea would be seen when a north east gale would howl through the Sutors, dashing the waves against the rocks of the North Sutor while the fury of the gale whipped up the waves, sending the white horses prancing towards the shore.

But the sea at its most beautiful is at sunset – those moments when the heavens are flooded with glorious brilliance of colour and the sun rays touch the sea, turning it to liquid gold and crimson – quite, quite beautiful.

Living By The Sea

I love Living by the Sea because I can play on the beach whenever I want. I find pretty things — pottery shells, fossils, stones and pebbles. Quite a lot of wildlife lives near the Sea, especially dolphins. I like paddling and running in and out of the waves, even when it is very cold. I like watching all the boats go by. Most of all I like watching the Sea from my window at home.

Lauren

Living By The Sea   By Eilidh

Living by the Sea,
is really nice to be.
When I ride my bike by,
the dolphins jump with me.

The Sun Shines brightley,
The Waves grow brighter.
If there's a Tsunami,
it's very likely,
As I bounce with a wave,
I'll have fun.
I look around,
At the golden Sand is where I gaze.

Living by the sea   Dylan

I like living by the sea, even the smell of it pleases me. its fun to paddle in when its hot. I like fishing for mackerel and cod. when its windy its wild and fierce. The waves fly right over the pier, The water it sprays in your face and leaves your lips with a salty taste When its snowy its calm and quiet thats when I really really love it. So young and old come and see its simply the best living By the sea.

Sea Children

by David Tallach

7 years in Cromarty

Tied to the ocean from birth,
Reef knots supplant the umbilical cords
Of the sea-children.

Playing around the harbour,
Boats painted in preparation
For the sea-children.

Sailing out for the first catch,
Drenched in the salt-spray
Are the sea-children.

Courting in low-walled cottages,
Wedding in the church with ancient gravestones,
Continuing the line of the sea-children.

Experienced now in the ways of the tides,
The caprice of wind and wave
That yield the herring to the sea-children.

Growing older in the same home-spun clothes
Their fathers wore
Before these sea-children.

Fateful howls the storm in a wild winter,
Tearing the vessel from bows to stern,
Taking the lives of its own sea-children.

Widow-black clangs the church bell,
A mourning mist descending,
To mark the passing of the sea-children.

Resting in the deep,
At peace with the waters they fought,
The ageless sea-children.

Bobby and Helen Hogg enjoying the sun in their Cromarty garden.
Photo courtesy of Bobby and Helen Hogg

The first mention of Bobby Hogg's forebears in the public annals of Cromarty is in the 16th century. They were boatmen and fishermen. Today in the early 21st century Bobby aged 87 is still in Cromarty and still has a boat, continuing half a millennium's association with the sea. His wife Helen (85) is a direct descendent of the polymath Hugh Miller, Cromarty's most celebrated son, underlining the importance of the family's DNA to Cromarty's story. Their house is the first port of call for many seeking to know more about Cromarty, its history and traditions which they both hold dearly. It is also a long established social thoroughfare.

Their son Robert, a former marine engineer, has inherited his father's maritime interests and spends much of his time restoring boats. He and his family live in a house in Cromarty's Fishertown which dates back to 1780 and used to house four fisher families. Robert's sister Rhona lives in what was the Cromarty Cottage Hospital, which looks up the Cromarty Firth to Ben Wyvis.

Bobby:

My father was a fisherman. My folk have always been fishermen, all the way back to Galilee. On my mother's side too. She was a Finlayson. But my great grandfather is buried up in the graveyard and his name was William Fiddler. His son is buried beside him and he is William Finlayson. At one time all the people called Fiddler in Cromarty changed their name to Finlayson. We do not know why and there is nothing in the church records to explain it. I think myself there must have been some infamous guy with the name Fiddler and the people didn't want to be associated with him. So they changed their name.

You see the fisherfolk were kind of God-fearing folk. You would never, ever hear them swear. When there had been a bad day there would be 20 or 30 men standing at the bottom of the Big Vennel, walking back and forward as fishermen do, but you wouldn't hear them swear.

Of course they would be talking in their own speech. You see when I was young we talked quite differently in the fishertown. We had this sort of patois, which had a good smattering of both Doric and Gaelic in it. But we would say 'thee' and 'thine'. The older ones were very biblical in their speech. I can remember my aunt saying things like "O Blessed Jesus". That would be followed by "O Holy one of Israel", then "O Great Redeemer" then "O Jacob". It wasn't blasphemy. It was just the way they spoke. But up the other end of Cromarty the people didn't have the patois. I remember going to school and coming home and telling my mother that the teacher couldn't speak properly. There were also people who had received no education. For example my mother's sister couldn't read or write. She would count by the score and measure with her thumb. She had some very strange phrases and expressions.

But there is hardly anyone else left who can speak the patois. There is my brother Gordon of course and there is the odd one or two who have a little bit of it. But that's all. It's quite sad in some ways. It still comes to me:

"At wid be scekan tiln ken?" That was just "What do you want to know?"

The names are still here. One of the oldest names in Cromarty is Hossack. They were fisherfolk as well. But you know, when I was young you could start along at the east end of the fishertown and every house along Church Street and Shore Street and every house up and down the lanes had somebody connected to the sea: fishermen, seamen, navy men. Now there is not one person there who goes to sea.

You could also start at the east end and work your way through the fishertown and every house would have a byname associated with it. There was nothing condescending about it. It was just practical. It was just the same way as on the islands where there are a lot of MacDonalds or Macleods, they will have different names to distinguish each other.

Well, when I was young there were five or six people with the name James Watson on Shore Street alone. In some families it would be the father's side that would give the byname; in others it would be the mother's. Our Robert is still known as 'Koka' and that came from his great, great granny. There wasn't a day at school he wasn't called that. But I wasn't. I was called 'Bolt'. It's a Shetland name. Don't ask me why.

The sea and fishing was everything then. My grandfather James Hogg, who was in his 60s, and his brother were drowned when they were out fishing. I was only two at the time so I don't remember it, but I remember people talking about it. It seems it was a fairly normal day in March, but the winds sprung up a southerly gale. They were in sailing boats of course at that time they were caught, just outside the Sutors. The bodies were never found.

The boats would go quite far out. That was why the women carried the men out to their boats. They couldn't go off for 24 hours soaking wet. They were good fishermen, but because the Cromarty men had good fishing on their doorstep they didn't go much into the nets or go after the herring the way the men from Avoch did. So they were better off for a long time. But as time went on the Avochies would be going through the Caledonian Canal and heading to the west after the fish and perhaps invested more than Cromarty.

But my dad when he came home after the war invested in a motor boat. He also got a seine net boat. But he got into buying and selling fish. He got himself a motor car and got somebody to teach him to drive. He would take fish to Beauly where a lot of the people were Roman Catholics and would eat fish on a Friday. He would go out in the car and sell fish all over. He would also send it down to the market in the likes of Manchester and had a shop. He did well. We were in the Paye House and Links House before that, and as a youth I never wanted for anything. But at the same time there was a great deal of poverty around Cromarty. There was hunger. There was no money about for fish. I was lucky in never experiencing it.

All my life was round fishing. I always thought I would go to sea or fishing, although my mother was always dead against it. She didn't live to know that I didn't go, although my oldest brother did.

After the First World War the trawlers started moving into the Moray Firth. They had been barred for a long time, but the likes of Belgians weren't barred and they used to come along in the cod season and they used to sweep the lot up. The Belgians used to get tremendous catches of cod in the Moray Firth. Furthermore, the development of the seine-netters and motors in the boats meant that the fish stocks in the Moray Firth were under pressure and so were the Cromarty boats. So much so that it is now more than 40 years since a haddock was caught here. We had been brought up on haddock. You used to say to your mother, "don't worry about the tea, I will go and catch it". I was talking to an angler recently who said he had barely caught one in 20 years of trying. The whiting and codlings disappeared as well. So did the graylings. You don't get them now and nobody now knows what a laithe looks like. The place used to be full of them.

I used to help my father in the boat but I was never a full-time fisherman. I went to work in a garage in Dingwall. But we all knew that the war was coming and I joined the RAF as a fitter, training pilots. We were used to seeing the planes around here and I talked to one or two who had gone to the air force. They influenced me, otherwise I would have gone to the navy. In fact I was seconded to the navy because the motor torpedo boats were getting new Packer engines in them. We were sent away to train on the Packers. I thought I was going to get to America, but instead I landed in England, in 'Pompey' (Portsmouth). I was at that for two years.

After the war I had been working in Yorkshire trying to learn about diesel engines, but I was courting Helen by then and the draw of that was much stronger than diesel!

Helen:

My father, James Cooper, was a grocer. He had a shop in the house that Wilf Taylor now has in Church Street. His father before him had come to Cromarty buying fish when the herring was at its height. He had stayed at Portmahomack but when he became ill he thought he should get something for his wife so they got the Shore Inn in Cromarty and once he died she carried on running it.

My mother meanwhile was a Johnstone, and her father was the chemist. Her great grandfather built this house we are in (in Denny Road). They lived here. My grandfather's wife's people were Rosses from Miller Lane. It was through them that I was descended from Hugh Miller. I was born in Denoon Villa.

My earliest memories of the sea was when we went swimming. We were very young when we were in the sea – great swimmers here. We weren't of the fisherfolk but we knew them, or knew of them.

I lived in Cromarty till 1943 when I went off to do nursing in the Royal Infirmary in Edinburgh. But I had to come home after I finished when the war was over to look after my mother and the rest of the family. That was when I met Bobby. We were coming out of the East Church. We had been in the same class at school but I hadn't seen him since he had left school more than 10 years earlier. Bobby had only got home to Cromarty twice during the war.

After we were married we went to Buckie and Bobby was working in a boat builder's. The whole community there would follow the fishing down to places like Yarmouth and Lowestoft at different times of the year. The men, women and even the minister would go. Later we went to Thurso on the Pentland Firth. Bobby was working first of all on fishing boats in the boatyard, then at Dounreay. But all the time I had to be going back to Cromarty because my mother wasn't well.

The furthest we ever lived from the sea was when we were in Leicester. We were about as far as you get from the sea and we were very conscious of that. We missed it awfully. You should ask Robert. We were in Leicester for 12 years 1959 to 1971 when Bobby was working for English Electric. We came back when he got a job at AI Welders who were looking for people. Then he went to Nigg so it was back to Cromarty. It was really good to be back. Nigg gave a lot of work.

When we were in Leicester Robert would come up here on holiday. When he left school he got himself an apprenticeship at AI Welders in Inverness, but the minute he had served his time he was off to sea with the Blue Funnel line as a marine engineer. He was in the Far East, Africa and up and down America. The sea was in his blood, but he got fed up and came home and ended up working at Nigg as well.

LIVING BY THE SEA

by Natalie

Living by the sea is nice.
Its cold and wet and really bright.
I like the lovely stuff inside.
There's crabs and fish and sometimes ice.
I walk along and pick up shells,
And on the beach the seaweed smells.

Living by the sea is harsh.
Its cold and rough and very dark.
At the sea there is sound,
Os big huge waves crashing down.
I love living by the sea
And so does everyone in town

The End

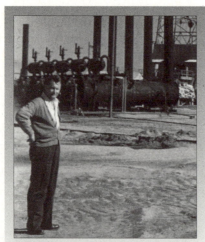

Bill Wren in Basra, Iraq, 1954. The oil drilling rig is a steam-driven Ideal 100. Photo courtesy of Bill Wren.

Ninety year old Bill Wren moved to Cromarty in 1978 after many years involved with the sea and the oil industry, both in Britain and overseas. He first came to the Cromarty Firth before the Second World War.

In 1937 I arrived in the Cromarty Firth on board the submarine HMS *Swordfish*. She wasn't an ocean-going sub; she was one of the smaller ones with a complement of about 32 men, including that most important person, the cook! I was one of four ERAs, that's to say Engine Room Artificers. We were the engineers that kept the Navy going.

I had joined the Navy in 1935 as a trainee ERA. After 6 months I 'passed out', (passed the Navy trade tests). My first commission was HMS *Valiant,* a battleship. We went to the Mediterranean: first stop Gibraltar, second stop Malta, through to Alexandria and joined the Fleet. From there we went round to the Suez Canal as guard ship, because the Italians had just started a war against Eritrea. After doing quite a while there we had to come up to Haifa in Palestine where the first Arab uprising against the Jewish settlers was. We were there for 10 months and the Navy took over the railways so I was one of the engineers from HMS *Valiant* on to the railways. We then trailed the railways up and down Palestine and then the Spanish Civil War broke out. HMS *Valiant* was the C-in-C (Commander in Chief) of the Mediterranean's draft ship, which he could send anywhere at any time without detaching it from the Fleet, so from Haifa we had to go up to Majorca as guard ship for British evacuees coming out of Spain to Majorca to be shipped out. We were there until January 1937.

Whilst we were in Alexandria a big submarine called The *Clyde* tied up alongside Valiant and there happened to be an ERA on there who was going through the school at the same time as me and I went down with him, had a chat and looked round the boat, and I thought 'that's for me'. So when we got back to Devonport in 1937 I volunteered for submarines and instead of going back to my home base, HMS *Pembroke*, Chatham, I was drafted round to HMS *Dolphin* at Gosport, commonly known as Fort Blockhouse. From there I did my training on a WWI submarine, the L26, and then passed out.

So, in 1937 we came up to the Cromarty Firth with the Fleet on a summer cruise, on the sub, HMS *Swordfish*. Our depot ship was HMS *Lucia*, a pre-war German passenger ship that had been captured and converted. Whilst we were up here at Invergordon we used to use the canteen there, which to me was a bit too noisy, so we either went to the Balblair Ferry Inn (which intrigued me because all the furniture had King George V's head on the backs of the chairs and on part of the table) or we would come to Cromarty, to the Royal Hotel. Incidentally, these two hotels and the other one in Cromarty – the Arms – they were all at that time government-owned.

If we came ashore like that, the depot ship supplied a launch which would go round the fleet and drop you off wherever you wanted to go. So we used to come to the Royal Hotel, and in those days if you had a florin (present day 10p) you could get two pints of beer, a dance in the Victoria Hall and on the way back to the ferry there used to be a fish and chip shop above old Bank House (where Derek and Margaret Matheson lived). So after the dance we used to go back down, get fish and chips and wait on the jetty until the launch came to collect us. One of the dances I was at in the Victoria Hall was on my 21st birthday, I remember that well.

We were in Singapore in September 1939 when we got the signal that war had been declared. We went straight back to Hong Kong, got live torpedoes on but not mines, refuelled, replenished everything and then left Hong Kong, went back to Singapore, crossed to Ceylon again, Aden, up through the Suez Canal and back to Alexandria. The depot ship HMS *Medway* was with us. There were 11 submarines altogether in the flotilla on the China Station. We all made our way back to Alexandria, our base. The China boats were all big ones: 1500, 1750 tons. The eastern part of the Mediterranean was deep so we could work that part, whereas the western part was shallow, so that's where the smaller boats from Malta and Gibraltar would work. We'd be at Alex on a three-week patrol and you'd be given a box (on a chart). Once you were in that box you did not stray from it, otherwise you were fair game from your neighbours, see what I mean? Friendly fire, that's right!

Every inch of spare space on the subs was loaded up with wooden cases of food. After the patrol we'd go into Malta and offload the food. (Malta was being blockaded by the Germans and was being starved.) We'd go into the harbour that was the submarine base at Malta, where the flotilla from Malta worked. We'd offload the food and the army's lorries would come and distribute it. On my sub, the *Rorqual,* where we carried the 50 mines along the outside, we used to fill up with drums of petrol, kerosene, so that we could then take fuel in as well. And then we would refuel and get stock, then it was back to a patrol for three weeks and then back to Alex, get tidied up, do your washing, air your bedding for about a week and then you were off again. I didn't get claustrophobic in subs. Anyone who did was out. I moved around a bit in the war, always in subs.

In 1950 I was working for the Iraq Petroleum Company and was transferred from the Basra area, Iraq, to Abu Dhabi. I was one of the engineers overseeing the contractors building a tanker loading terminal. It was sheer desert back from the coastline except that behind was a huge salt dome, 370ft high. We built a road up to the top of this salt dome first of all, from the shoreline, levelled the plain out and that's where we built our tanks.

The oil used to come down from there through meters out to the tankers that were moored three miles offshore. They were fed by two 18 inch underwater pipelines to each berth and we could load two tankers three miles out to sea. My office was right on the shoreline where I could watch the sea hawks fishing. The company built a little harbour which the Arab dhows used to come into and unload fish in the area of Jebal Dahhna – this was where we built the tanker loading terminal. It was 70 miles across the desert from Abu Dhabi town.

After a tanker had finished loading we used to stop the meters and read off how much had been loaded in tons. During loading, the temperature and gravity of the oil had to be taken every hour and centrifuged to see if there was any sediment in it. If so, that was noted. At the end of the run from start to finishing loading the tanker, these figures were then collated and laid out. They would then go on to the ship's captain's papers and the main office in Abu Dhabi. After that we used to shut down maybe for a few hours and then another tanker would come in and during a month we could load up to 24 tankers. One month in 1955 I loaded over one and a quarter million tons of oil! The tankers would get their papers but the owners would then radio them and tell them to go to Aden or Gibraltar for wireless orders where they would go and offload it. We had no oil spills during my time there. I left in 1966.

I came to live in Cromarty in 1978 because of my affinity for Cromarty and the Black Isle. Then, by a strange coincidence, it wasn't long after that, in 1983, that the oil terminal was built at Nigg. In the local press they were advertising for people who knew all about tank farms, tanker loading and all that. But they had to live on that side of the Firth, and anyway, by then I'd had enough – I was retired.

Orkney or Bust

by George Selvester

George Selvester, Commodore of Cromarty
Boat Club 1996-2004
Photo courtesy of George Selvester.

Born in Edinburgh in 1943, marine engineer George Selvester moved to Cromarty in 1993 and served as Commodore of the Cromarty Boat Club 1996–2004.

The Cromarty Boat Club's 'Commodore's Cruise' which I introduced a couple of years after the club was formed in 1996 has been increasing in popularity every year.

The success of the 2002 trip through the Caledonian Canal to the West Coast strengthened my resolve to go for Orkney in 2003. A meeting was called in January and nine boat owners agreed it was *Orkney or Bust!* With cancellations and dropouts en route, only three boats were left to sail all the way to Orkney. The following is from my log of that voyage.

Saturday 7th June 2003

Jock Wingate in his *Heart of Gold,* who has spent the night alongside in the harbour, is up and about, just finishing his breakfast. Alex Davidson, his crew, has already arrived and they are just about ready for the start.

I too had left *Fat Sam* in the harbour overnight to make it easier to get aboard with our gear. Gavin Meldrum and his crew Rod Duncan arrive about ten minutes later and are quickly out to their mooring to prepare *Polar Wind* for the trip. My son Steve and I are ready for sailing by the time the last crew, Peter Baxter and 'Pug' Peterson of *Norseman* arrive. Another boat, *Wigeon,* skippered by Bill Paterson with crew of Neil Brooker, has left an hour ahead of us.

There is no wind at all and the water is mirror-like, the reflections on the water of both the North and South Sutor look spectacular. When we live in such close proximity to natural beauty we tend to take it for granted; however, mornings like this have a way of reminding you how lucky you are to be living in such surroundings.

Log reading 4397.5. Forecast winds light to variable SW. Course to steer from Buss Bank. 030 degrees.

The trip to Lybster is pretty boring as we have to motor most of the way due to the lack of wind. For a period of around an hour a slight breeze gets up from the south-west which allows me to use my spinnaker; however this is short-lived and we are soon back to the Suzuki and its five horses.

All the boats have spread out a bit but we remain in sight of each other all day, arriving at Lybster at about 15-minute intervals, with the exception of Bill Paterson who has arrived an hour before any of the rest of us. *Fat Sam* passes the light at the end of the pier at exactly 1530.

High-sided hills around Lybster mean radio signals are non-existent within the harbour area so anyone needing to contact home has to climb the steep road up to the village in order to get the use of their mobile phones. It is a strange coincidence that the signal seems to appear right outside the nearest pub, Bayview Hotel. As we are so close we might as well have a drink. What a hard life this is!

After a couple more beers we are all feeling the effects of such an early start and one by one make our way back to the boats.

I am in bed by 2200.

Log Reading :4433.1 Distance covered today 35NM.

Sunday 8th June

The facilities at Lybster are excellent since the opening of the Heritage Centre: £5 gets your boat in the harbour for the night and the use of the showers/toilets and washing machine/drier. It was on our previous visits here that we got the idea to install similar facilities at our tower in Cromarty.

After everyone is suitably washed and fed, the two boats *(Heart of Gold & Norseman)* that are returning to Cromarty slip their lines and bid us farewell. *Fat Sam, Polar Wind* and *Wigeon* set sail to Wick at 0830.

We are forced by very light winds to resort to the motors again. We arrive at Wick at around 1130, replenish our petrol tanks and fill all the spare cans we have in case we have to motor all the way! On completion of this important task we all feel that we deserve a pint and a meal and so retire to the Moorings pub.

We leave at the agreed time of 1530, in the hope that we can reach Duncansby Head at a favourable state of the tide, and this I reckon to be at 1930. The wind has picked up slightly, enough to fill the spinnaker, but again without much headway so once again we have to resort to motor power.

Polar Wind and *Fat Sam* arrive ahead of *Wigeon* and note that there are lobster pots dotted around Duncansby Head, which give us a good indication of the strength of the tide. We are just managing to hold 'station' against the tide if we sit at half throttle. This way we can face back toward *Wigeon* and monitor his progress. We watch as he grows from a dot on the horizon to the recognisable form of a Snapdragon 21. We started out together and we are now going to cross the dreaded Pentland Firth together! We are now 45 minutes later than we had anticipated. We pass into the Pentland Firth at 2015.

With the distinct lack of wind we do not get any of the famous 'overfalls', but can plainly see all the currents and eddies that make this stretch of water so dangerous. The tidal atlas has been studied very carefully and we are able to negotiate the crossing with very little difficulty at all. However, there is the occasional tidal race that picks up the boat and moves it several feet in a sideways motion. This makes us a little concerned at first but we seem to get used to it quickly and soon learn to spot the dodgy bits as we approach them.

We head in the direction of Lother Rock with the Pentland Skerries two miles off to starboard. As we get closer to Lother Rock the tide then continues to take us, carrying us midway between South Ronaldsay and the island of Swona. At this point the log on *Fat Sam* is registering 4.5 knots and the GPS tells me we are doing 8.5 over the ground.

I feel that as Commodore I am responsible for the safety of the crossing and I fuss like a mother hen with the other two boats. I seem to be getting further ahead of them all the time and am concerned. At one point I feel they are both too close to the island of Swona and warn them that if they do not steer toward South Ronaldsay they are in danger of the tide carrying them round North Head and down to the 'Merry Men of Mey'. Their response is a change in direction from *Wigeon* with nothing said and a similar change of course from *Polar Wind* followed by a radio transmission, which I regret to say I am unable to decipher.

After passing the entrance to Widewall Bay it is relatively straightforward and I round Hoxa Head just before 2200. Here again there are lots of lobster pots, the difference being that they have very long lines attached. I am weaving in and out of them hoping that my propeller will not foul on these ridiculously long lines. Once clear, I look back to see the other two coming round Hoxa Head and I radio a warning about the pots.

2215: Steve goes forward to drop the anchor in St Margaret's Hope Bay and within half an hour we are all rafted up together and having a celebratory drink. I have no idea how long we stay up as I cannot recall going to bed.

Log Reading: 4466.7 total distance covered today 33.6 NM.

Monday 9th June

When I wake up in the morning I lie for a long while, in no hurry to rise. The last two days have been quite long and I feel quite tired, even after a night's sleep. I eventually get up around 0800 and am amazed to find the cockpit strewn with empty Guinness cans and wine bottles. I clear away all the rubbish and make a cup of tea during which time the gas runs out.

I inflate the rubber dinghy and go in search of somewhere to buy gas. Just my luck: nearest stockist is a good sail away in Stromness. I ferry all the crews back and forth from their boats to the shore and we spend a couple of hours walking round the few shops in the town and send some postcards home.

Eventually Neil's 'nose' for finding an open hostelry works well and upon finding the bar of the Murray Arms Hotel open and dispensing the nectar, we enter and introduce ourselves to the co-owner and barmaid, Barbara. The bar is dotted with memorabilia of the wrecks that are widely scattered in Scapa Flow following the scuttling of the German Fleet. There are also various pieces of diving equipment. There is a strange object on the shelf behind the bar which, Barbara explains, is to test the lung strength of divers, and she asks us if anyone would like to try it out. Steve and I both smell a rat and look at each other, then decline. Rod and Gavin make no move to try it and Neil sits with a knowing smirk on his face. Poor old Bill, unaware of what is going on, says he will have a go, takes a deep breath and blows into it with all the power he can muster. A white cloud envelopes him as the rest of us fall about laughing. I think Bill is blushing, but nobody can really tell as his face is completely covered in talcum powder! We do not stay too long in the bar (I think Bill is eager to go). We set sail for Stromness at 1230.

Wind is better than it has been of late at around force 4, and although it is from the north-west and against us, we sail up Scapa Flow. *Polar Wind* chooses to sail to the north-east of the Flow (perhaps to look at the marker buoy for the wreck of the Royal Oak which was sunk in Scapa Bay). Whatever the reason, he is chased away by a pilot boat to allow a tanker to manoeuvre.

Bill is now out of sight, having pressed on again under power as I do eventually, in order to get the gas before the shop shuts. This becomes a real race against time. As I motor toward Stromness Harbour, Neil comes on the radio to give me directions and within ten minutes I am tied up alongside *Wigeon*. It is now 1650 and I have to find the shop with the empty gas bottle in my hand. I make it with a couple of minutes to spare.

I wander back to the boat (via the Royal Hotel) in time to witness *Polar Wind* berthing at 1800. The wind has changed and he manages to sail all the way up to the harbour entrance. Well done, Gavin! This is just as well for he is still having problems with his engine.

I am sure the reader can guess where we go next. I am so tired though and retire to bed at 2030, very early for me.

Log Reading: 4480.5 total distance covered today 13.8 NM.

Tuesday 10th June

I sleep right through until 0815, which is very unlike me; I must have badly needed the sleep. We decide upon a rest day and stay over for another night here. We visit Kirkwall by bus where I buy a new battery as the old one is not holding its charge. We have to sample a couple of the bars as we are in the capital, and then get the bus back to Stromness. Neil and Steve decide to cook a meal for everyone, which turns out to be decidedly average.

We have earlier made an arrangement with the Ferry Inn to use their shower facilities at £1.50 per head, and we feel it is only fair that we spend some time in the bar afterwards. We have all agreed that today was worthwhile as we needed the rest. We sit down to plan for tomorrow.

With Bill's continuing engine problems they set out a couple of hours ahead of Gavin and me. They are also planning to go down through Gutter Sound on the inside of the island of Fara; this is a slightly shorter route. They then intend dropping anchor in Long Hope Bay to await the arrival of *Fat Sam* and *Polar Wind* at the Sound of Hoxa, having sailed back down the Scapa Flow, where we would join up and cross the Firth again together.

Wednesday 11th June

By the time we surface, Bill and Neil have gone.

The forecast for today is ideal for crossing the Pentland. It is 1030 when we slip anchor and head out into Hoy Sound. Now it's the turn of Gavin's engine to play up. He has just informed me that he sees no signs of water coming through the cooling jacket. Luckily the wind is sufficient for him to sail out of trouble. The tide in the sound is against us and is trying to force us out into the Atlantic. We are making a little headway but it is painfully slow. The wind is very good; we are on a reach doing 5 knots across the water but only half a knot across the ground.

I move in as close to the shore as I dare to cut down the effect of the tide and radio Gavin to tell him to use this tactic. It takes almost an hour to reach Scapa Flow but by the time we do, the wind has strengthened considerably and swung round to be on our stern. We are making excellent progress now and the tide is no longer a problem. I set a course to sail close to the 'Barrel of Butter', which is about one third of the way across the Flow.

With Steve now at the helm it gives me a chance to look at the charts and tidal atlas again, just to double check I have the timing right. I take a closer look at the route *Wigeon* plans to take and realise that at the time they intend coming out of Cantick Sound they will run into a severe tide race with overfalls. It might be okay in light winds, but the way the wind is rising I think it might be prudent for them to make for Widewall Bay on South Ronaldsay and wait for us there. I try to radio but can't raise them so get them on the mobile and explain the situation. I also tell them about Gavin's outboard problem and promise to keep them up to date with events. They are going to up anchor and go to Widewall Bay as I suggested.

As we approach the 'Barrel of Butter', Steve is having difficulty keeping us on a straight course; the boat wants to veer off to starboard. I have to take a full reef in the main and take in half of the rolling foresail. Once this is done, we are still doing 7-8 knots. I reckon the wind strength to be at least a force six, gusting seven, perhaps even more!

All the diving boats are hurrying for sheltered water.

Bill phones back to say they are just entering Widewall Bay and that the wind is, as Bill puts it, "piping up". Another call from Gavin tells us that Rod has the engine in bits in the cockpit and does not think he can rebuild it when the boat is tossing about. He is however attempting it. I ask him to keep me informed as we have to make a decision whether or not to go for a crossing today. We also have to tell Bill what we are doing.

At 1230 Gavin radios again to say that the task of rebuilding his outboard is impossible in these conditions; we have to find shelter to complete the job. St Margaret's Hope is probably the safest bet now. I call Bill on his mobile, telling him of the change of plans once more. They don't sound too pleased about the whole situation but when I remind them there is a pub at the anchorage, they quickly accept the inevitable and up anchor once more and head round to St Margaret's Hope Bay.

Steve goes forward to drop the anchor in the bay and I note the time at 1350. Gavin and Rod get down to putting together their engine whilst Bill and Neil go off in search of a petrol station. Once all the chores are completed, petrol stowed away etc, the engine on *Polar Wind* is given a test run and as it seems to be okay we retire to the Murray Arms for the now mandatory pint.

We are all back on board by 1700 and make our meals in the separate boats, exchanging the odd derogatory remark to each other across the water, there being only 35 to 40 feet between each of the craft. We have a party aboard tonight with Gavin bringing the bottle of gin that had been left on board the boat when he bought *Polar Wind*. There are copious amounts of the said gin, lager, Guinness and Export dispatched and our hearty laughter must sound strange to the landlubbers ashore. When it comes time to retire I am quite surprised that Gavin and Rod do not end up capsizing their dinghy on the way back to their own boat.

Log Reading 4493.9 total distance covered 13.4 NM.

Thursday 12th June

Wind is very light again this morning and is forecast to be variable 2-3. I check my calculation again and determine that the best time for us to enter the Pentland Firth is 1530. We have breakfast, put away the inflatable and sail round to Widewall Bay where we wait for the time to pass. An hour later we are tucked inside the bay. The wind has dropped to no more than a whisper, so we raft all three boats on one anchor and sit down to discuss the meaning of life!

We also discuss Bill's engine and decide to take a closer look at it. One spark plug has signs that it has not been working at all so another is fitted and bingo! It is now firing on **two** cylinders. The next hour is spent 'ribbing' Bill and exhausting every imaginable pun, much to the annoyance of Bill until he says, "OK, enough is enough!" So we drop the subject.

With the wind now gone completely I figure we should leave at 1500, so off we go. *Wigeon* now has the bow wave of a destroyer! Round two of the sick jokes and puns now that we are out of his reach.

The crossing is flat calm. Gavin gives us a call on the radio at one point to say that they have spotted a killer whale off the south tip of South Ronaldsay. I am reading 5 knots on the log and 9 knots over the ground and in no time we are passing Duncansby Head, then Noss Head at 1830 and eventually into Wick for 1930.

I am in bed by 2230.

Log Reading: 4515.2 total distance covered today 21.3 NM.

Friday 13th June

Everyone is up and about for 0700 and we are anxious to get on our way. Steve is leaving today, so I now have to sail single-handed on the way home.

By the time we sail out of the harbour it is after 0930. We have lost half the tide and although we are making good time at the start, we soon slow down as the tide weakens its influence in our direction. The wind is straight on the nose and although it has been forecast to be 3-4 it is a lot stronger than that. There is quite a heavy sea running and I have a fully reefed main and only half the foresail out, sailing close-hauled. God, this is hard work.

By the time we get to Clythe Head the tide has turned against us and the wind is now in excess of force 7, probably nearer 8. The waves are pounding against my bows and every time I get some headway a wave hits the boat and stops it almost completely. I sail for a good while but can see that the relative bearing on Clythe Head is remaining the same, so I decide to go on power. This too proves to be extremely difficult.

I can hear Gavin on the radio but I cannot let go the helm to answer him. I find out later that he is asking if we should pull into Lybster for a spot of lunch!

The wind is ferocious now; the only thing the forecast got right today was the bloody date! It takes me over three hours to go the two miles from Clythe Head to Lybster and the wind is still increasing.

Extremely glad to get into Lybster at 1430.

Sit in the pub (where else would one go?) and discuss the plan for tomorrow. If the wind has dropped sufficiently we will leave very early and try to get all the way home; if it is still windy we will settle for Helmsdale. Bill volunteers to get up at the crack of dawn and if conditions are right we will make as early a start as we can.

Do not have much to drink tonight as we are all pooped and ready for going home.

Log Reading: 4527.9 total distance covered today 12.7NM.

Saturday 14th June

Bill duly rises as first light comes in and, seeing that the wind has dropped completely, wakes the rest of us. I get a forecast from the radio: "winds light and variable", 1-2. It's either blowing so hard the seagulls are flying backwards or there is no wind at all. What a country we live in!

We are on our way by 0515, a good time as the tide is against us but is almost spent. In another hour it will be in our favour.

We resign ourselves to the fact that we are going to spend another day under power and set a course for home. The good thing about this kind of weather and having to motor when I am sailing single-handed, is that it's a simple task to put the kettle on for a brew, but to tell the truth it is an extremely boring way of making headway.

Because the navigation is so simple in these conditions I tend to become a bit complacent about taking a fix or an estimated position (these are very familiar waters to me). I am relaxing at the helm watching the world go by when I am interrupted by the sound of Bill's voice on the VHF, pointing out that he is running short of fuel. *Polar Wind* responds by suggesting we head for Portmahomack to replenish our supplies. I then suggest that the easiest option lies with calling in to Helmsdale as the tide would be fine for entering. This is unanimously agreed upon and the radios fall silent for a while. About ten minutes later I hear Rod saying, "Fat Sam, where are you going"?

"Helmsdale of course", I reply.

"What's that off to starboard then?" says Rod.

"Berriedale," say I, with indignant confidence. " I think not!" comes the cheeky reply.

I get out my binoculars and look at the town two miles off to starboard. My God, it is Helmsdale! I will never be allowed to live this down.

Rather than engage in further conversation (to make excuses would be futile), I simply alter course by 90 degrees to starboard and follow the transit line into the harbour. Any thoughts that they will be sympathetic and not raise the subject are quickly dispelled when they appear in the harbour entrance behind me…. Let's just say they give me a lot of stick!

We quickly fill the cans with petrol and are back aboard the boats inside half an hour. We take a further fifteen minutes to make a cup of soup and a roll, then head back out into the Moray Firth at 0945.

There is still insufficient wind to sail so we continue to motor toward Tarbet Ness. Bill is obviously more confident with the extra petrol onboard and is well ahead of the others by the time we reach the Lighthouse at Tarbet Ness. Shortly after I pass the Point the wind gets up from north-east and I am able to fly the spinnaker again. This lasts until I am just passing the 'Three Kings'.

Jock in *Heart of Gold* has come out to meet us and is sailing at first, but as he reaches me at the cardinal mark the wind dies again. Both he and I take down our sails to motor yet again. The tide has turned some time ago and the ebb is pushing us back. As I pass between the Sutors there is a sudden squall that brings with it a good wind which I could use to enter Cromarty in a blaze of glory with all sails up. To tell the truth I cannot be bothered and in any case nobody would notice. I carry on with the motor the last mile home.

It is a great feeling to have achieved our goals; an even greater feeling is spending the night in my own bed.

Log Reading: 4560.0 total distance covered today 32.1 NM.

Total Distance covered on the whole trip was 162 Nautical Miles

Douglas Matheson.
Photo by John McNaught.

Douglas Matheson (86), a retired maths and physics teacher, belongs to Cromarty. He met his wife Jess (86), a native of Fochabers, while they were both teaching in Insch in Aberdeenshire. They lived 10 years in Invergordon, then went to the North Island of New Zealand near the port of Gisborne for three years. They returned to Scotland in 1963 with their two sons and two daughters to allow them to go to university here.

They came back to Cromarty, then Grantown on Spey and Forres. This was before returning to Cromarty to live opposite the town's lighthouse which Douglas tended through his retirement until 2006. For most of his life he lived within sight of the sea, but he still clearly recalls his first real experience of it, or rather in it.

I must have been about three or four at the time. My father had a shop in Bank Street and there were a lot of old tyres about. I selected one and that was my gird. Tyres weren't as heavy as they are now. Using my hand to guide it rather than a stick, I got it going well down Bank Street towards the harbour. But the slope increased, as did the speed of the gird and away we went right over the grassy bank beside the pier, over a pile of seaweed, across a stretch of stones and into a strip of sand where a wave came and knocked me flying back into the seaweed.

The tyre carried on into the sea. I remember being shocked at the sheer power of the wave, the way it knocked me back. There were some people watching but they didn't give me a hand. I retrieved the tyre and went home. Meet the sea!

The shed that Bobby Hogg has now, was the slaughter-house. We used to play nearby. There were two or three naval cannons lying to the east of it along the Links. They probably dated from the sailing ships of the early 19th century or late 18th. They had stepped supports for the cannons. They fired our young imaginations.

Just over the bank from the guns were enormous piles of seaweed so we used to have fights there after constructing forts from the seaweed. It was a great place for us to play. During the Second World War the cannons were taken away for scrap metal.

This is going back to the 1920s. We played a lot down on the shore then. A lot of the local fisherboys were marvellous with a sling. I never really mastered it, but they could throw stones tremendous distances and used to be accurate. They would have competitions to see how far they could get. The sling was the tongue of an old boot with two strings and a hole in it to hold the stone.

There were lots of children in the fishertown then and to me, as a young boy, it was dangerous country. There used to be fights, the east end versus the west end. It had nothing to do with parental status, just geography. There was a fountain in front of Forsyth House on the High Street; that marked the dividing line. When the curfew bell sounded at 8pm everybody would disappear whether there was fighting or whether we were all playing football, often the same teams. The police spurred us on our way home.

Cromarty Harbour was a very busy place in the early 1920s. All the cargo for the Cromarty end of the Black Isle came by boat. There was a company called Coastline Seaways. It was based in Leith and used to come with stores every week. Commercial travellers would precede her and take orders from all round the area. The boat would tie up at the pier and unload all the supplies. The local carrier, Jock Shepherd, would go from the pier delivering to all the shops and taking cases for anyone who had travelled north by train and bus.

At the end of the First World War a lot of timber was still being exported from Cromarty. In front of the Royal Hotel there used to be huge timber-carrying bogies with four or six horses. They would be taking wood to the pier to be loaded on to ships. The timber came from the Sutor and other estates on the Black Isle. It was a great shame because there were some lovely trees. The men driving the timber bogies would invariably visit the Royal Hotel for refreshment.

At that time there were still about 60 fishing boats in Cromarty, and each boat would have had a crew of four or five. Now there are three.

The fishwives were a marvellous set of ladies. I remember seeing them carry their men to the boats on their backs so they wouldn't get wet before they went out fishing. The boats would lie in the harbour, while others would be pulled up on the Links at night.

But the women wouldn't carry them back ashore when they returned three or four hours later. The boats would leave at dawn and would be back in Cromarty before 10 in the morning. The fishwives would fill their creels and race round the town to catch their customers. I remember them coming to my door. We lived above the present day Londis shop then, and it frequently happened that two fishwives would arrive with their creels of fish at the front door at the same time. My mother would be scared to go down to avoid the squabble. She would wait until the victor came up the stairs. The fishwives would come into the scullery and clean the fish and then on to their next port of call. Some would go out to the country to the farms. They would almost run out to Jemimaville. I had an aunty who lived in Culbo, 10 miles away. Sometimes the fishwives would arrive there on foot with their fish for sale. They would barter with the farmers and their wives: fish for eggs, tatties, turnips and oatmeal.

I remember one, a woman who was known as Annaig Sponge. She went out to Culbo once, sold her fish and was coming back when she stopped at Newhall bridge, about five miles from Cromarty. My grandfather was the Blacksmith at Newhall. For a rest she backed up to the wall of the bridge and let her creel rest on the parapet. A local man played a trick on her by creeping up behind and putting a big stone in her creel. To the amazement of everybody she just pulled it up on to her back and away she trotted.

Some of the Cromarty fisherfolk would take the bus to Dingwall with their creels. All the salmon from here would go by ferry boat to Invergordon and then by train down to London.

In the afternoons the women used to bait the lines then go to the woods to gather a 'burden': twigs and branches for the night's fire.

The men would go out at low tide and dig for lugworm. The fisher folk were great characters. They were all known by their bynames. I think at one time 45% of the town were Watsons. Then there were the Hossacks. All the Hossacks in Scotland could be traced back to Cromarty.

All the fishing was line fishing. After the First World War seine-netters began to appear and the local fishermen used to get mad, swearing and shouting at them. Some of the Avoch fishermen bought seine-netters but the Cromarty men never did. I remember hearing the Avoch men criticising their Cromarty counterparts for not investing in the new fishing boats, saying 'Whatever money they get, it goes against the wall of the Royal Hotel.' The Avoch men would save and invest in new boats. It was not that Avoch harbour was better than Cromarty. It wasn't. It dried out. But there was a railway at Avoch to get the fish to Inverness. If there had been a railway to Cromarty, perhaps the fishing industry could have continued longer.

The seine-netters got the blame for the decline of the Cromarty fishery. I remember some fishermen in the Buckie area bragging about how they had killed the fishing in Cromarty.

Cromarty depended on the sea. Cromarty was the sea, but my people were of the land. Although they never went to sea, the Cromarty Firth was the ever-present backcloth to our lives. Never more so than when the fleet used to come in. It would fill up the firth. Invergordon couldn't cope with the big battleships and they would lie off Cromarty in the deep water. You would get aircraft carriers as well. Cromarty used to look forward to them coming. From when the first ship put her anchor down, men would start coming ashore to Cromarty for cross-country running, hundreds of them. They would go as far as Newhall and then come back. Other boats would take officers to Nigg to play golf. Then you would get football teams coming ashore to play here, rugby teams too. There would be three pitches on the Links and one on Victoria Park. Football was also played along at the Reeds and on ground up at the top of the Denny, on what used to be called Jock's Field.

There used to be a naval outfitters where the Cromarty Arms is now and he used to open up for the fleet in the spring and the autumn, and he must have done well enough then to last the rest of the year.

I went away to Glasgow University in 1938 to do Maths and Physics but the war came and I joined the army. At one point I was stationed in England at Retford, which was far from the sea, as far as I had ever been. I didn't like it at all. Later, I trained in Combined Operations which involved sea-work. After retiring to Cromarty I served over 20 years as Lighthouse Keeper and 5 years as Auxiliary Coastguard in charge of the local search and rescue team. So I ended my productive career back at the sea which had knocked me for six so many years ago.

Reflections of the 1750s Customs House caught in the old fish store sign.
Photo by Fran Tilbrook.

The Sea is fun,
The Sea is Wet
The Sea Can handle a Speeding jet.

Some people Swim.
Some people paddle.
People just Can Stay there for 24 hours.

The children have Ice cream.
The Children have fun.
The Children Come to the Sea Side
When theres Sun.

Molly

Bill Campbell with a 19th century Royal Navy carronade cannon found at Newton Farm in 1945. Photo by Calum Davidson.

Asked what it was like to farm beside the sea, Bill Campbell of Newton Farm had the following thoughts which focus less on the maritime conditions and rather more on the underlying geology of Cromarty.

We came to Newton Farm from Caithness in 1945 when I was ten years old.

We're near the sea but it's an inland arm of the sea so it's fairly sheltered, maybe not like if you were facing the north – out on the Aberdeenshire or Banffshire coast where you're more exposed. . Farmers there would be more aware of the sea.

The only advantage here of being close to the sea is that you're at sea level; the higher you go, the more you're into the snow and frost level. Apart from that, we're not bothered with sea fogs: Aberdeenshire, Banffshire, they can get fogs for days on end that really affect the harvest. Arable farming in that area is curtailed by maybe a week of misty, foggy weather. If you're harvesting, for example, you can't do anything because fog is damp. Foggy day: no sunshine, no wind. But for us, we've probably got a kind climate here in the Inner Moray Firth. The Gulf Stream goes right round the north and there's an eddy, a big whirlpool in the Moray Firth and we get a slight bit of warmth from that. But honestly, as far as farming near the sea goes, at least where we are situated, I can't see much advantage apart from altitude, or lack of, and the fact that it keeps a little snow away.

We would be all arable here if every field lent itself to that job. But because the land nearest the sea is undulating and steep in places it's not all that suitable for machinery – hence the cattle and sheep. There is something peculiar to the east coast: Sutherland-shire, the Inner Moray Firth area – cobalt deficiency. Now what causes that, how it's in one particular area and not in another, I do not know. Before the days that they really discovered what it was, it was dreadful. You'd get the shepherd throwing in the towel and leaving because the sheep were just melting away; it was called 'pine', and you didn't know what was wrong with them. We called them 'piners', like a runt, and that was to do with lack of cobalt.

We've got very poor draining land here. You've got sort of plough depth and then we're sitting on clay that's almost impervious to water. So you get a very wet spell, the plough depth fills up with water and there's nowhere for it to go. So it makes the crops quite sick or it makes our job difficult to do. If we were on lighter, sandy soil then it would be easier for arable farming but it could dry out in a very dry summer. We're up from the raised beach, so we're really sitting on red clay. Probably the red stone of this house would have been clay many thousands of years ago, and then it would have been consolidated, compacted. If you dig deep enough you come to red sandstone.

As far as I know there was a quarry down below Newton here, down below Neilston, the old cottage. There's no sign of it now but you do see red sandstone and occasional off-cuts. The barges used to come in, the tide went down, they loaded the sandstone and then when the tide came in again they were floated out and they went to Fort George. So some of the stone for the building of Fort George in the 1760s came from just below this farm.

The Cromarty Song

This song, written by Jane Mackay and Margaret Ritchie in 1966, is fast becoming part of the age-old oral tradition of sea songs. Especially popular with the Fourways Club (for the over-60s), young people too are now carrying on the tradition.

They call me a wanderer,
Wherever I roam,
And yet my thoughts linger
In my old Highland home.
It's the home of my childhood,
The land of my birth,
It's a wee place in Scotland,
On the Cromarty Firth.

All the world's seven wonders,
Not one can compare
To the view from the Sutor;
It really is rare.
As you stand midst the heather,
Far below you can see
All the beauty of Scotland,
In my Cromarty.

Now the people are happy,
So friendly and kind.
It really does grieve you
To leave them behind.
But young folk must grow up
And then must depart,
But the home of their childhood
Lies deep in their heart.

And now I must leave you,
And bid you adieu.
My feet they will lead me
To pastures anew.
But my heart's in the Highlands,
In the town by the sea,
In the home of my childhood,
My own Cromarty.

In The sky

On The sea

under THE

under THE

SEA

SEA

Sea Poam

The waves are rushing by. Crashing and howling loudly

Boats are struggling up and down up and down. Through the waves splish, splash.

Sharks are getting hungry looking at all the fish.

The storm is coming down hard

Niamh

Ronald Young at the controls of the Cromarty-Nigg ferry, Cromarty Rose.
Photo by Calum Davidson.

Skipper of the *Cromarty Rose* ferry boat for more than a decade, Ronald Young, 34, was clearly born to go to sea, starting work on oil boats the day he left school.

I got an 'O' Level in seamanship and nautical knowledge from Fortrose Academy when I was 15. Sandy Mackenzie was the teacher. He was the second coxswain of the Invergordon lifeboat and he was also a technical, woodwork and metalwork teacher. We used to get three hours of seamanship a week. The school had a dozen Mirror dinghies and a 26ft launch called *Red Wing*. It was great for the Avochies, who were going to follow their families into the fishing. I can honestly say without that background I would never have gone near a boat. The school no longer teaches seamanship, which is a pity and a sign of the times. It has long since sold off all its boats. I think the janitor bought the launch.

I also used days off school to get out to sea. 'Study leave' I called it! I left school at 15, on Friday 30th May 1988 and started night-shift on one of the oil boats at half past six the same day at Invergordon. Things really got started when I was a cellar boy in The Byre. Whenever he came in, I kept getting on to Derrick MacDonald of MacDonald Ferries to let me have a run. I had a moustache, a very small moustache, which made me look older and made sure I didn't get asked too many questions, and I probably got away with a lot more than I should have at that age.

Derrick's father was old Somerled MacDonald, the farmer at Sheeppark Farm, who operated the Invergordon-Balblair ferry service, and then when the oil business got under way they ran all the workboats to the rigs in the firth. These were stand-by boats: cargo boats, tugs, landing craft – anything between 30ft and 95 ft. They were all named after birds. The first job I had was on a boat called *Gannet,* before I left school! My friend Erwin Roehling was the skipper. Then I was on *Tharos,* a semi-submersible support rig which was later involved with the Piper Alpha disaster. I was crewing with my uncle 'Buller' Mackay, and Erwin. Then there was *Merlin* – that was my company car, so to speak! I used to take it home and tie it up next to the fishing boats in the harbour at night, then take it to Invergordon in the morning. It was a 40ft tug, mostly taking passengers to the rigs. I was also skipper of *Skua,* a solid steel workboat, and the rig was *Trident 10,* a jack-up rig sitting on top of *Kawala* barge in the wet dock at Invergordon. The pay was £1.60 an hour and I was loaded at the end of the week. I was doing 80 or 90 hours a week. At one point I was working more hours than my father, my mother and my older brother put together. I would go to work at 5 o'clock in the morning and not get home till 10 o'clock at night. I can remember times getting a call at 10 at night to go back to Invergordon. From the age of 16, I got £3.20 an hour. I didn't have any time for drinks, parties, girls. Most people that age have pop singers' posters all over the wall. I had RNLI lifeboat posters. I knew every single boat in the MacDonald Ferries fleet – their length, their width, their horsepower, all at the top of my head.

I don't drink, never have done. I just don't like the taste of it. I think I can count on one hand all the times I've touched alcohol. There was the games room upstairs at the Royal was all I did. So my wages stayed more or less intact. I gave the money to my mam and she banked it for us.

Oh they were lively times, taxi service for the rigs. There were a few guys you knew, drinkers you'd drop off at the rig, and you knew fine you'd be back an hour or two later to take them ashore again, they'd been sent off by the rig boss, the OIM (Offshore Installation Manager).

Some of the OIMs were little Hitlers. We weren't caring — we were getting the money for the runs. The heaviest drinkers, who would have been drinking right through the night and only had an hour or two's sleep, they'd be scaffolders. Don't get me wrong – they were the greatest guys to work with. Nothing was a problem with them. Although they were party animals, blazing drunk, they'd always be polite, good with you; they were family, the scaffolders. As far as rig crews themselves were concerned, they were mostly very good too. With rigs stacked in the Firth for a long time, you'd get on first name terms with them.

When I finished on the rig boats I worked briefly at the fish farm here and at Ardersier for a short time, then the fishing over at Gairloch, but I wasn't keen on that. Then, it was 1993, I got a phone call saying there was a new owner of the Cromarty-Nigg ferry. My contact said, "There's a guy coming up from the Department of Transport (DTI) next Friday, do you fancy sitting your boatman's licence?" "Yeah, okay," I said.

The DTI man was Captain MacFarlane, a Shetlander, a big, huge old tall man. We were sat at the big conference table in the Cromarty Firth Port Authority office, and there was this model boat. He pointed: "This is you, and that's a ship towing a rig. Who has the right of way, what lights would be displayed?" and so on. One of the questions I always remember was, "You are leaving Invergordon proceeding east, and on your starboard side you see a yellow flashing light. Mr Young, what would that light be?" I was still young, quite nervous, and to try and break the ice, I said, quick as a flash, "A snowplough on the Black Isle."

He pulled his glasses down, looked over the top of them, and said: "Is that your final answer?" I says, "No, it would be a hovercraft." "Thank you very much," he says.

One question he kept asking, and I didn't know the answer, and he said if you don't get it I've got to fail yer: "What fog signal does a vessel under 50 metres make when it's at anchor?" I said, "I don't know, do I guess?" Old MacFarlane said: "You must know, you have to answer it. I will give you five minutes. I will leave the room and come back."

So I sat and thought desperately. At anchor, it had to be one of three: a horn, a gong, or a bell. The penny dropped: it was the bell. He said, "There you go," and signed the form, and that was it. It's a lot harder now. These days a boatmaster's certificate involves a three-day sea survival course, two-day firefighting, four-day first aid, a full day VHF radio operator's course, your oral and practical exam. A couple of weeks, and probably a couple of grand. Not an hour in the Port Authority office and £45 as it was when I did it.

Cromarty Rose

So there I was on *Cromarty Rose,* and here I still am, fourteen years later. Yeah, I've had a few accidents. In the early days I was too busy yapping, and she got stuck on the slipway and stayed there until the next tide. I've broken down in the middle of the channel, due to a lot of seawater getting into the diesel. We managed to make it into Nigg. I had a farmer's wife with two young kids on board, one in a pushchair, one barely walking, and she was white as a ghost. She said "I'm never coming back."

On a good day, a nice calm day, if you wanted to learn anything about boat handling you probably couldn't pick a better boat. But if there's a strong tide or wind, anything you know about seamanship can be thrown out the window. You are always taught you should be head into the wind or head into the tide or whatever, but the way it is with the ferry you are always side on and there's nothing you can do about it. It's a landing craft boat, and if you don't get it right on the slipway approach, you could fill with water in seconds. The first shot I had, it was on the Nigg side which is much tougher than Cromarty. Cromarty, you know where the wind is, and the tide, but at Nigg, it's so close to the deep channel. You've got wind and tide and you've got eddies as well. The tide is ebbing in the middle but coming in at the shore, so the Nigg waters swirl round. And then you've got groundswell; because the channel's so deep the water wants to come on to the beach so quick and then you're surfing. Nigg's the nightmare. Well, my first time, it was October, pitch dark and a howling westerly gale. I was the most relaxed I've ever been because I thought, there's no way I'm gonna do this, this boats's gonna end up on the beach and I'll be able to walk off and get a taxi home. And the landing went just fine.

You do 44 landings a day and you never do the same one twice, because by the time you get back to the slip the tide's further up or further out; spring tides you are hitting the bottom. There's no easy steering. We're conventional: we've got two propellers, two rudders and you've got no control of the bow, so you have to line your bow up first. You use your ramp as a brake, lowering it quick on to the slip so it holds your bow there while you work her stern up into the weather, or the tide, or whatever.

She's an old bucket sometimes but you've got to love her, I suppose. When she's coming in with the ramp still up she looks like somebody just belted her in the nose but she's a good toy to play with, she really is. She's underpowered and she traps a lot of wind. When there's a birl of ebb tide and a strong westerly wind, it can take an hour to get from Nigg to Cromarty, y'know. I've seen us get from Cromarty to Nigg in less than three minutes and then 48 to get home.

When Nigg Yard was on the go, it didn't matter what the weather was, you crossed for the men, although you wouldn't for the normal day-to-day passengers. You made a special effort for the Nigg men. I remember going in to Nigg at three in the morning, the back shift coming home, and it was a right hoolie of a gale and the swell was so large you were seeing all of the slip one minute and none of it the next. We went in on the top of a wave and landed on the top of the slip and the wave fell away and left us there, high and dry, propellers turning in mid-air. That was pure luck, because if I'd misjudged this wave it would have slammed us down hard on the top of the slip and burst the boat open. There was nothing to do with skill at all, just guess, hope and pray. All the Nigg men ran on real quick, and then another wave came in and lifted us up and took us off again.

First shift we would leave Cromarty at half six in the morning, then staff, half seven. The shuttle would start at 8.00a.m. Then at half past four we took the back shift over; at quarter past five we took the day shift home. The back shift would be taken at the back of three in the morning except Fridays when they finished at eleven. Nigg work went up and down and more or less finished by 2000.

I never had any trouble with any of the workmen. We've had to carry a few boys out of "The Piggery" (Nigg pub) to help out. When it was rough, they all knew not to take their bikes, because they wouldn't have time to run on with them. They'd leave the bikes at the top of the slip. They'd give you a bit of stick if you were ever late. The biggest worrier of the whole lot when we were on the water was my father Andy, he'd always be up in the wheelhouse with me when it was rough.

I have never ever been afraid on the ferry. Always wonder what I'll do if an engine fails. You could have a flexi coupling in the shaft might break, or the engine could pack in for some reason or another. She handles like a pig with one engine down. There's nothing worse. You can only turn her one way then. Takes half the firth to turn her in.

Visitors normally come in waves – it's all Australians one year, then Italians. The last two years it's been all Brits, very few foreigners at all. Kids make your day. You say to them, "You take it across," and they get their photograph taken and they love it. On a good day you can tell them to turn three spogues of the wheel to the left or right and they think they're steering the boat in! The rudders aren't hardly moving, you are actually taking it in on the engines, but they think they're doing it, right into the slip, it's great.

A lot of old war service people come up, an incredible number. They hear the name on the shipping forecast and they think 'I must go up there again'. We have the charity walkers and cyclists doing the John O'Groats to Land's End thing.

A few years ago there were army guys going all over Scotland's war memorials laying wreaths, and we picked them up so they could lay a wreath over the wreck of *Natal* about 7 in the morning.

The public often ask, what chances do you have of seeing dolphins, and I tell them the same chances as the moon at night! You can see them at the top, middle or bottom of the tide, first thing in the morning or last thing at night. There's no pattern at all. What we do when we sight them is call Sarah Pern of the EcoVentures dolphin cruises up on the radio. We keep her updated, especially when we saw the minke whale last summer. We thought at first it was a big tree and we should warn her. It was just off the Cromarty Harbour, and we thought we'd tell Sarah to watch out for this tree; then the tree disappeared, meaning, the whale dived.

The crew is always two: the skipper and the deckie. It's quite funny how it's turned full circle, with Erwin Roehling having been the skipper on the rig boats when I left school and I was the deckhand; now it's the other way round on *Cromarty Rose;* I'm the skipper and Erwin's the deckhand.

I think the ferry's getting busier since Johnny Henderson took it over. During the winter we seem to get a fair bit of rig work too, which is quite good. We are the only boat in the firth with a passenger licence for 50, whereas all the MacDonald boats can only carry up to 12. When we had a lot of rigs in, in the 1990s, we thought the *Stena* Rigs were the worst, we called them much cheapness because they tended to lie out a couple of miles outside the Sutors to save money on berthing fees. *Cromarty Rose,* best of luck to her, is not the fastest ship in the fleet, so it was a long steam out and you might be home putting the kettle on and get a phone call saying "Oh there's a bloke just turned up at the harbour wanting out." *Jack Bates* was the best, just off the harbour. We knew all the guys on *Jack Bates,* and the whole crew were just fantastic with us. Anything that we wanted, it was no bother.

Why were there so many rigs coming in and out back in the 90s? Well, say a rig is inspection surveyed by Shell for a contract. Three months later, its next job is for BP. BP will survey it again; three months later, Conoco hires it – same all over again. For an inspection you'd have a full complement aboard I would think, which could be anything up to 90 men. If a rig's just in to lay-up, it would be a skeleton crew of between four and eight.

The reason we've had so few rigs in the last couple of years is the high price of oil. The one in the firth now is getting made seaworthy to go to India, I believe. I think as long as the oil lasts, the firth will never be empty of rigs because it's such a good anchorage.

But they do nothing for Cromarty's economy. There's nobody from here employed on these rigs. There's only one side of the firth working – everything's done out of Invergordon. The Port Authority when they had the lease of the harbour, they never did anything with it. Okay, they put that stupid ugly Bailey bridge on, but that was it. The Port Authority states they pile money back into the communities round the firth. Well, they're not spending a penny of it round here that I can see. They could be putting money into subsidy for the ferry, but they say it's not an economic development, which is all wrong really. An all-year, north-south route would be a lifeline for the Black Isle and the Nigg side.

Nor do we see any benefit from the liners. They take all the passengers off to Dunrobin and Loch Ness. What's Loch Ness compared with Cromarty? Why take all the cruise parties there and none of them here? Loch Ness, it's like walking down a lobby, just a stretch of water with hills either side. There's a lot more character in the town, and there's a lot more character in The Sutors than there is in Loch Ness. The visitors could be bussed from Invergordon to Nigg, then cross on the ferry and have a look round. Then their bus could take them on through the Black Isle and wherever. I'm sure there's a lot of people who'd find that more fun than just going down Loch Ness.

I often think Cromarty's a thorn in the side of Highland Council. They've got to look after the West Coast, that's supposed to be God's country as they see it, but Cromarty's out the way, out at the end.

The future of *Cromarty Rose?* She's over 21 years old now. Her hull is sound, as good as the day she left the shipyard really; all she's got is a lot of superficial rust. Mechanically, she could do with a serious overhaul: engines, rampwork, gear, turning table and maybe a bit of modernising in the wheelhouse. She's probably the only boat afloat today that still works on a compass and compass only. No radar, no echo-sounder, no GPS – the most technological thing on the ferry is my mobile phone.

I could maybe do with a change some time. It does get a bit boring. The practical boat-handling side is always a challenge though, and the craic with the passengers can be good.

On a good day, the sea is the biggest invite on the planet. I've gone to Newcastle from here in one of the tugs and it was like a mill-pond the whole way down and through the night, sitting on the afterdeck looking at the moon – it was just absolutely great. Just a sheen for miles and miles. I see all sorts of nightfall on the *Rose;* in the season we're sailing before sunrise and after dark.

I can't swim, still can't swim a stroke. If you asked a hundred skippers, I think you'd find 90 of them would say 'oh, I don't like getting wet'.

I don't believe much in the superstitions of the sea myself but there's still a fair bit of it about. You can't mention pigs on the boat, you've got to say curly tails or grunters. There was a farmer over by Fearn who came on board with a rubber pig's head as a cover for his towing hitch, and Michael (Roehling) said "we can't let you sail with that on". You've got fisher boats which will only turn the direction the sun goes. Salmon are either 'red fish' or 'queer fellas'; rabbits you call 'underground jiggers' or 'thumpers'. You shouldn't whistle or you'd raise too much wind. You're not allowed Swan Vesta matches on board – very unlucky – and if you meet the minister, you've got to turn round and go home.

One thing we still do is pay our dues to the sea. We get coppers from passengers and put them into a jar, and at the end of the season we throw the jar in the middle. We say, we're making our living by the sea, so thanks, we're giving you something back.

Living by the Sea

Living by the Sea
is the best place to be
where lots of happy people live together
happily.
people come from far and wide
to look at the spectacular sea
all the wonders of this place and all its
history.
The harbour with its fishing boats
the smell of all the fish that was
caught very early that day and ended
up on your dish.
The wonders of the sea
the beauty and the appeal
are the dolphins, crabs, sea birds
and the bobbing of a seal.
Every day is different
there is so much to see
the changes of the weather
Living by the sea in Cromarty.
— by Lily

The View from Navity

by Ian McCrae

8 years at Navity, Cromarty

At Navity I overlook the Moray Firth and the ever-changing sea and sky never fails to delight.

Both in the morning and in the evening at sunrise and sunset it is almost like a picture by Turner, and the colours in the clouds outdo any spectacle in the theatre or cinema.

To walk along the shore provides an unending variety of seabirds and occasional glimpses of dolphins add to the interest.

In summer when liners call at Invergordon I marvel at how these giant, and to my mind rather ugly, ships – they almost invariably look like floating blocks of flats – manage to stay afloat and not turn turtle.

As a small boy I always loved the sea and would stay in it for hours, to my parents' consternation. Nowadays I find it somewhat chilly and prefer to look at it rather than get in it.

Living by the Sea

by Paige

I have lived in Cromarty all my life. I love living by the sea and we are really lucky. Most people have to travel to get to a beach but not us. When it is hot we put our swimming stuff on and run down to the sea and swim. When I was little I have fond memories of collecting shells and different stones. I love finding skimming stones and seeing how many times it will skim. I also love seeing all the different boats coming in. My favourite one is the boat with the face on it, so I am really lucky to live in Cromarty and it is a great place to grow up.

Rosie Newman filming sea birds.   Photo by Calum Davidson.

An artist working in various media, based at The Stables Studios, Rosie Newman moved to Cromarty in the early 90s. One of her latest projects is to film seabirds, in particular flocks of knots: waders frequently seen along the Cromarty Firth from Udale Bay to Cromarty. Her passion for the sea is strictly limited to observing it, having experienced a terrifying ferry crossing some time ago.

A few years ago when I lived in Bayview Crescent, I used to take my cup of tea down to the beach and watch the knot birds and one day I thought 'Wow, they're amazing' – the way they appear and disappear. I was quite interested in wallpaper at the time and I loved this idea of making a room of wallpaper – bringing the outside inside – by filming and then projecting the images on to a wall. It could have been all birds, but then I started filming other things like the wind, shadows, and also close-ups of the sea - the movement – I like the idea of movement, the patterns in the environment.

And so I spent a couple of days with a friend, driving up and down by Jemimaville, trying to find the knots – then I realised that they're so hard to film! You're only looking through this tiny lens and you think you've got them and of course, the thing about them that is so amazing is that they just turn and disappear. They're great, the way they come and go. When the birds land they're invisible because they're camouflaged and look like the pebbles. One of the things that's beautiful about them is their white under-belly, and when they turn all together, that's what you see. I love the patterns they make. There's something magical about them but they are hard to film.

When looking at the sea I like the impermanence of the view: it's always changing. You could never make an identical copy of it. Thinking about permanence and impermanence, it's semi-permanent in the sense that the water itself has always been here and always will be (though environmental changes make it into steam or ice etc) but there's something kind of ancient about looking at the sea; it doesn't have the clutter that's involved in buildings or any connotations associated with man-made things. It's like staring at mountains, it's very meditative.

But I'm also terrified of the sea. One of my worst experiences ever was on the *Cromarty Rose*. It must have been about eight years ago. A friend and I had gone over to Nigg to cycle and then the weather changed. We were on the ferry on the way back when a massive storm arose. Everyone went downstairs in the cabin, but I thought 'I'm not staying down here. I'm going to the top because at least you can jump in!' so I was holding on to the bars of the deck with white knuckles and the ferry was going right up and then down and the sea opened, you could almost see the floor of the sea, it was like a roller coaster – thankfully there were no cars on it. I was soaking wet because the waves came right over you and people downstairs were screaming their heads off. (I still feel worked up, just thinking about it.) I remember being really terrified but then there was one moment when I just completely relaxed and I thought 'I know I'm going to die' and I looked at the sea and thought 'I'm going to be in there soon but at least it'll be quick', and all that kind of thing – it was that bad. But we made it! When we got back, loads of people from Cromarty were out on the Links, because it had obviously looked amazing. The skipper was great. He kept saying 'Ach, it's fine, don't worry about it.' It took me ages to get back on the ferry again. I got really freaked out by it. Maybe I drowned in a past life!

People were here initially because of the sea; it brought life – fishing and then the oil industry, which was what brought my family here in the 70s, looking for work, from Liverpool, where the sea was important too, with its trade and so on. I couldn't live away from the sea, even though I'm scared of it. When I went to America recently to an artists' colony I was very pleased we were right on the beach, not landlocked. I brought shells from Cromarty with me and made them into necklaces for all the artists (from all over the world) and they all wanted one and wore them with pride. So now artists from America, Japan, France, Macedonia and China etc have shells from Cromarty beach. The sea gives you a feeling of freedom, of space and I suddenly felt at home there. That sense of the familiar is so comforting.

Steps

by Jacqui Ross (née Winton)

born in Cromarty

Dad built me steps

We live on the seafront
Separated from the beach
By the high sea wall, so
Dad built me steps

Years of endless fun
Beachcombing, paddling and
Learning to swim, because
Dad built me steps

Thirty years on; a storm
Washed my steps away
His grandchildren were upset
Their access to the beach was gone
Dad built them steps

The Magic Dolphin

by Iris Winton

born and bred in Cromarty

I have four granddaughters: two now adult, two aged 11 and 8. I often had them for 'sleepovers' and of course at bedtime they always wanted a story. They did not want any story from a book – they had heard them all before, so I had to make one up – the favourite being about a dolphin. Living on the sea front the children spent all summer on the beach and often saw the dolphins jumping out of the water – hence this story.

'One sunny day the girls were on the beach making sand castles. All of a sudden they heard a great 'whoosh'! Looking round, they saw a huge dolphin had landed at the water's edge. This was a magic dolphin. It asked the children if they would like to have some fun by coming for a ride with him. They thought, 'how can this happen?' But out of the dolphin's back came a golden ladder. They were amazed to see this and hurried up it. When they got inside the dolphin it was like paradise. There were all sorts of sweets, cakes, ices and games, and the bottom of the dolphin was glass so they could see the bottom of the firth and were mesmerized, looking at the sea creatures: fish, lobsters, crabs and the seaweed swaying back and forth. They had a trip to Invergordon and saw Billy (Dad to two of the girls) then a trip to Nigg and saw Ronnie (Dad to the other pair). They decided they would like to go out towards the Sutors, so the dolphin headed that way. He dived deeper and deeper and after a while the children squealed with delight as there, sitting on a huge golden rock, was the most beautiful mermaid with long golden hair and her tail curled round the rock. She was singing softly. It was now time to head for home. The dolphin sped toward Cromarty and swam alongside the ferryboat, many other dolphins joining him. The children were landed safely on the beach and couldn't wait to tell their parents about the wonderful adventure they had had.'

(The girls were usually asleep by now!)

I spent many hours sitting on 'The Steps' watching the children paddling, making sand castles, collecting shells or playing 'smashie' (you smash up sandstone with a hard stone and add water to make a paste which you then use for various things like 'tanning' your legs). Their days on the beach were indeed full of wonder. They are so blessed to live by the sea.

Home Thoughts

by Karen Meikle

11 years in Cromarty

During my life I have never lived far from the sea. I was born near St Andrews and spent my childhood, after a brief spell in Cupar, Fife, in Montrose. Memories of beach walks along the Angus coastline remain strong, whatever the season. In my teenage years my family moved north to Saltburn near Invergordon, and the sound of the sea filled my ears and my moods changed with the tides. I used to look across the Firth at Cromarty and watch the evening light fade on Cromarty's white houses. The jewel in the crown of Scottish vernacular architecture lured me to visit with family and friends, and in 1995 I bought 14 Forsyth Place.

In the last eleven years I have been away from my familiar coastline: in 1997-98 I swapped it for the flatness and cornfields of Indiana. I spent a year teaching in an American high school, living amongst soya beans, corn and hogs – quite a contrast to tatties, oilseed rape and sheep! Then in 2002-3 my partner and I spent ten months travelling the globe. At times we lived by the sea: on the coast of Queensland, in New Zealand (where we saw the most southerly bottlenose dolphin) and in Chile.

Yet I was always glad to return home – to walk the shoreline, to embrace the salty winds, to imagine Cromarty's past – hearing the industry of the fishertown, the merchants and even the huzzahs from the emigrants.

There is a magical quality to living by the sea – its rhythm and movement can bring peace and harmony as well as fear. I love early summer mornings when the sea fills my nostrils and laps ashore; I dread stormy nights when the sea rages at me and mankind.

Gazing down from the South Sutor, our town makes herself known – stretching out to welcome her neighbour, the Firth – and I realise how fortunate I am to live on this peninsula.